Not Another
Indian Guru

Copyright © 2021 Ajay Kavasseri
All Rights Reserved.

Cover Artwork by Ameya Ajay

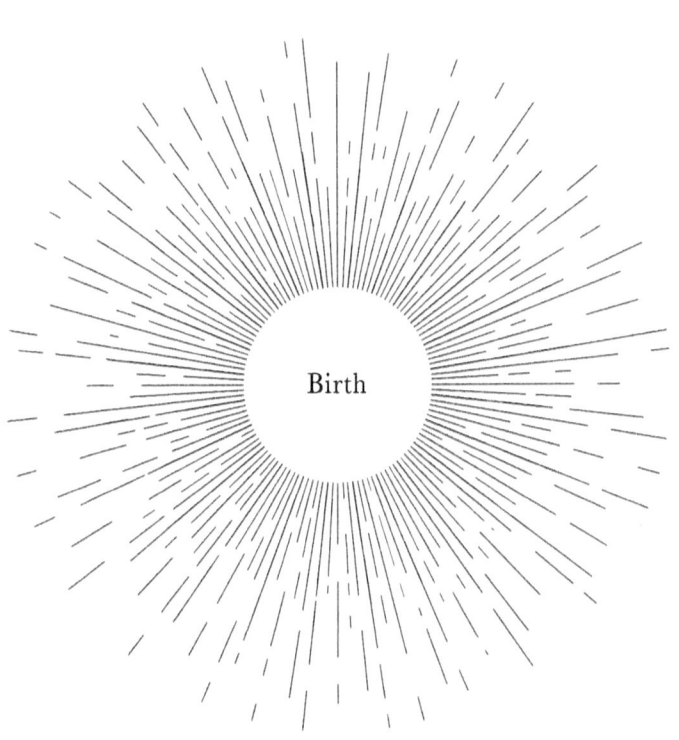

I wake up one morning and see something wonderful, something beautiful, something truly real, a panacea and I cannot believe it. What do I do? I ask myself. I'm so excited that I want to share this with someone. You're in my house sleeping, so I quietly walk up to you and whisper in your ear: "good morning, get up". You don't move. I gently tap you, "hey, wake up, I want to tell you something". No response. I now shake you a little, and with excitement in my voice say: "hey, you gotta see this". You say "mmm" and go back to sleep. I get a little sad and plead: "please, you're really missing something". Nothing from you. Now I get a little agitated, "c'mon, I really want you to see this!" All I get from you is a "what?!" By now I'm fed up, on the brink of tears, I shake you: "wake up, get up!" "Go away, let me sleep!" I'm stunned. I walk away in disbelief. I leave you alone. I go write a book.

But then why write a book? I'm only journaling, not specifically writing a book. Although, if it does eventuate, it would merely be a manifestation or by-product of different ideas, intuitions, opinions, perceptions, and also frustrations and contradictions articulated and put together on paper using a technology or tool called language – English in this case. And all these are nothing but insights and thoughts that have occurred to me. Unsure of their origin, this egoic self or "I" just happen to be the one a) heeding and listening to them, b) perceiving and trying to understand them, and then c) interpreting and expressing them with the use of images and symbols i.e. a linguistic script. There are a few pieces that I've picked straight out of a magazine I used to run and write for, called SELF, and some from my YouTube channel.

Although someone said that when you learn, teach – the intention here is not to proselytise or preach, and not even to inspire or motivate. It is only an attempt at articulating, or rather documenting some of the understanding I've had on different aspects over the past many years of self-enquiry, questioning, contemplating and experiencing, not to mention experimenting and testing.

You may find this book like an abstract jigsaw puzzle: there are several individual pieces or parts that need to be taken into account, that come together cohesively, not necessarily to solve the grand mystery of life but rather to get some understanding of it. As you read through this journal, please note that there are no bottom lines, which is the only bottom line.

I guess I don't need to do a disclaimer, since this is a personal journal. However I do wish to state that by applying any or all suggestions in this book, you agree to take 100% responsibility for all actions and consequences. Advice, if any, is provided without warranty, and is definitely not medical advice. Also, references of "you" are meant to be "one", unless I'm ranting :-)

I've been on a journey, call it an odyssey, of Personal Development and Self-enquiry which began in March 2012.

It started when I was reading a book by Robin Sharma called *The Monk Who Sold His Ferrari*. It was an interesting book on personal development but with a spiritual flavour – that I immensely enjoyed. There was a particular chapter early in the book, where the author compared the mind to a garden, and that we had to stand guard at the gate of this garden and let only the very best information enter. He then went on to state that one truly couldn't afford the luxury of a negative thought. Not even one. Yes, not even one! That turned my life around. I began to ponder and think about all the things I'd been pondering and thinking about, most of which were negative. And that's when I made a commitment to myself – to try not let a negative thought enter this garden of my mind. Not even one!

Thus began my journey. I stopped using negative language, expressions or words, and even stopped saying the word "no" for a period. I had become a yes-man. My mind was in an amazing space of exploration and curiosity, enthusiasm and positivity, and I was living and breathing these things all the time. This phase carried on for a few years. I was reading a lot of books on personal development, on change, on spirituality and on success; and I was doing all this reading to develop this so-called "inner" self. More about that later.

I was reading biographies and also listening to the audio version of the documentary *The Secret* every day. Then I was handed a book written by Eckhart Tolle called *The Power of Now*, and that book made a significant impact in the way I was functioning. From this book I learnt about awareness and consciousness and being in the present moment: to let go of the past and not worry about the future – to basically be in the Now.

I also began connecting with nature a lot. I was observing and paying close attention to trees and plants, birds, insects, the moon and stars and wanted to get more and more connected with everything nature. "Why me? Why now?" were two of my most FAQ for the first couple of years. At this point, I can't help but talk about tears – they would flow all the time. I would bawl my eyes out, all out of pure joy and ecstasy, regardless of what I was doing, where I was, or whom I was with. The littlest of things would trigger the outpouring of tears – sometimes quite uncontrollably. This went on for about 2-3 years. And there was a particular sensation in my body, blissful to say the least, that lasted until early 2018. More about that later.

During these initial years, I did verbal affirmations every morning, like "I am confident, I am courageous, I am disciplined" and "I am more than I appear to be, all the world's strength and power rests inside me". I even created an acronym, HEAD, that stood for humility, enthusiasm, appreciation, and discipline, which I was following, or at least strongly intending to do so, all the time. I was becoming more loving, more tolerant and very forgiving – not just to my family and friends but to everyone and everything.

Around this time I got my first smartphone and was using it to watch a lot of personal development YouTube videos. I was also listening to Napoleon Hill and getting inspired by everything Hill had to say about having a definite major purpose in life, going the extra mile at work, maintaining self-discipline and being enthusiastic all the time.

Living with enthusiasm – it is truly a tremendous way of being. There was one particular episode by Hill called Applied Faith, which would pep me up every time I felt I was succumbing to my pre-epiphany conditioning. Hill taught me how trust, confidence and belief were important qualities to have – that everything on the outside was fine, and that every situation was actually shaping and moving me towards my major purpose in life – to fully awaken.

To pursue this new learning, I went on to enrol in one of Robin Sharma's online courses on personal development and success. While I was doing all this, my performance at work, at least on a personal level, was becoming better. But more importantly, my interactions with everyone was developing and improving.

I got deeply into journaling, and was in a state of such immense enthusiasm and spirit that I was speaking (even publicly) to more and more people about this journey. I wanted to share all these fantastic ideas that were occurring to me so that others could also lead a wonderful and ecstatic life.

I went on to publish a magazine on Apple Newsstand called Self – Source of Energy, Love and Fun. I was constantly getting new insights and ideas, especially in the mornings, and I would share all those ideas with my wife and daughter, and a few others.

Another book – actually a trilogy by Dr David Hawkins – that took me to a whole new level was *Power vs Force*, followed by *Eye of the I*, and *I*. I was absolutely blown away by how anybody could reach such exalted levels of awareness and even become enlightened, which prompted me to take up a course in Kinesiology. This was a phase of love, joy and peace, and I even had a sort of a mystical experience – vision of Jesus, Krishna, Buddha and Mohammad. More about that later.

Around this time, I was beginning to get intrigued about my physiology and the body that I was in, which led me to further contemplate on the true inner self. Everything the body was doing was based on what the true self was doing. I began to understand things like, "I am not this body, I am what is deeply situated somewhere or even everywhere in the body".

More about that later…

21.10.2020. After an 11-week hiatus, due to the Covid-19 lockdown, I was able to go back to work today. I would regard this time off as one of the best I've ever had in my working career. If not for this break, I wouldn't have been able to make a start on this book, which I've been thinking of putting together for the past several years.

Writing this book has been a kind of release for me. It's a liberation but also a vent. Not only are many of my frustrations and annoyances finding expression here, but even my sincere love and authenticity. What I really want from the deepest part of my Self is for everyone to quickly sort out all their egoic and survival needs and desires, and then start their own odyssey into self-actualising and spirituality.

Here's the epiphanic excerpt from Robin Sharma's *The Monk Who Sold His Ferrari* I read in March 2012 that got me started on this journey:

To live life to the fullest, you must stand guard at the gate of your garden and let only the very best information enter. You truly cannot afford the luxury of a negative thought – not even one. The most joyful, dynamic and contented people of this world are no different from you or me in terms of their makeup. We are all flesh and bones. We all come from the same universal source. However, the ones who do more than just exist, the ones who fan the flames of their human potential and truly savour the magical dance of life do different things than those whose lives are ordinary. Foremost among the things that they do is adopt a positive paradigm about their world and all that is in it.

So, this all started out merely as a personal development or self improvement exercise which then, as with any kind of research, evolved into enquiry about some deeper existential questions relating to spirituality, the self, reality, epistemology, perspectives and alike. During the initial period of this journey, I never heard any voices of the naysayers or the critics. I was so full of myself, and into giving free advice, that I didn't even bother listening.

However, as time went on and my quest to understand the nature of existence, life and the self grew stronger, I slowly started to hear them. From almost everywhere. I would feel some sort of resistance coming from people, they would argue and debate about a lot of these things – and it was coming, not so much from work colleagues or acquaintances, but from friends and family members. I failed to understand why anyone would take offence to the things I was talking about or suggesting. Why wasn't anyone else doing the things I was doing, or thinking the way I was thinking? Was it because I had changed, or because they were not willing to change? It's thanks to all the reading, learning and researching that the messages started to become loud and clear; that it's quite uncommon for someone to a) take such a path, b) delve so deeply into it, c) make it a full-time obsession, and d) keep doing it for so many years. I also realised that if I couldn't develop a thicker skin or withstand being misunderstood, ridiculed or criticised, then I would have to just forget about playing my part in making the world a little more aware and conscious.

Even this book! It may be difficult for someone who knows me personally to not only read it, but to stomach everything that's being said here. Just because they're coming from me – Ajay. If a well-known teacher, preacher or guru said the very same things it would quite easily be accepted. But you see, I am one of you, a nobody, and how dare I talk all wise and learned!

Look, I get it. I can totally appreciate how hard it can be for the ego to submit to, or acknowledge the merit, if any, of the things that are being said here, especially because some of them can sound profound or sagacious. And god forbid if anyone happens to get an epiphany or realisation from this book, the ego might have to give credit to this nobody! Which is still not as herculean a task as to let me know that they read the book in the first place.

As I've been on this journey of awakening and actualising, there have been two people who've always stood by me and encouraged me all along - in fact they still continue to support and encourage me – my wife and my daughter. If not for their ongoing reassurance, especially during the initial years and my lowest points, I would not have been able to pursue any personal development work, let alone self-enquiry and spiritual work. That being said, I don't want to totally undermine the support of a few others who were around me during the initial years. But I must say, as I went deeper down the rabbit hole I did lose connections and interactions with many of them – which I couldn't appreciate then but do now. That's just how it is. Many of you (I am tempted to say all of you but I'll give a fraction the benefit of the doubt) have a very myopic view of family, friendships, relationships, community, and of the world, not to mention of reality, truth and consciousness, therefore I don't expect you to fully comprehend what I'm trying to say here. But to the fraction who do get it, I take my hat off.

So while on the one hand I want to express my gratitude to the girls, on the other I feel I'm depreciating or devaluing all their backing by "saying" thanks.

This book does not have a beginning, nor does it have an end. This book does not have a "title", nor do any of its chapters a heading. That's how the book of life is. We like to think that birth is the beginning of life, and death the end; that each aspect of life has a title or a heading like education, career, family, finance, travel, hobbies etc. However, each aspect is actually holonic and interlinked with each other, all through you – the central character in your book or your story. You are the protagonist in that story – not your partner, your child, parents, friends, colleagues or even your pet. There's only one person in your life and that is you. Even if you sacrifice your entire life for someone else, it is you that is doing the sacrificing. You are the one leading your life, not anyone else.

"In case of a cabin decompression, put on your own oxygen mask first before assisting others, even if they're your own children and family members".

You can't help others if you don't take care of yourself first. What if, in life, you put on your own metaphorical oxygen mask first? Not because you're selfish, but because if you do, you can do more for others. How can you contribute your talent, your creativity and intelligence if you're gasping for breath? If you fall apart, you become someone else's burden. On this flight called life, we're all headed in the same direction, and to the same destination – it ends the same for everybody. So there's nothing wrong in putting on your own mask first. And once you've done that, you can start helping.

One thing I can say with certainty is that once you're on the path of self-discovery and actualisation, every aspect of your life will start to change; your involvement and devotion in all pursuits, regardless of the activity, will become intense and more enjoyable. You'll tend to put significant effort in the pursuit of excellence in everything you do, no matter what it is that you're doing – not to mention that you will even have a stronger sense of purpose and meaning to life.

Having said that, you will also be tested more than ever. Even if one day you feel as though you're on top of the world, it could change anytime. Always be prepared for the good times and the bad. Keep faith and keep working on yourself. Slow down and do not expect quick results. Your time will come.

Life tends to always unfold in chapters and phases. And if you're actively pursuing actualisation or if you're on the path of spirituality, then you're more likely to become aware of such stages. I actually didn't understand the concept of phases until I was in my 5th year of this odyssey, which is when I gave each phase certain words that I had been living by during that period. Some chapters lasted only a few months, while some a few years. Following are the phases I've been in so far, since March 2012 (in chronological order):

Thoughts, feelings, actions
Self, success, significance
Love, joy, peace
Inclusion, acceptance, curiosity
Balance, freedom, flexibility
Evolution, language, illusion
Frustration, nihilism, introversion
Non-duality, environment, purpose

Here are some of the teachers who have taught and continue to teach me on various subjects, such as personal development, spirituality, consciousness, religion, the self, non-duality, reality, mysticism, truth, mind-body, and more:

Robin Sharma
Rhonda Byrne – *The Secret*
Napoleon Hill
Dr Wayne Dyer
Jim Rohn
Dr David Hawkins
Alan Watts
Lao Tsu – *Tao Te Ching*
J Krishnamurti
Nisargadatta Maharaj
Eckhart Tolle
Dr Deepak Chopra
Krishna – *Bhagavad Gita*
Dr Joe Dispenza
Sadhguru
Leo Gura – actualized.org

I believe it's important that we seek, connect with, and learn from the sages, gurus and mystics, who are living examples of people that have found their true self. It's also important that we learn and practise some good meditation techniques that will help us discipline our monkey mind and ground ourselves in *being*. Then it's also important to start having conversations with others about our path and endeavour, and even provide suggestions – for it's the teacher who learns the most.

Importantly, you don't need to stop living your "normal" life – you can continue with family life, socialising, doing your job, pursuing your hobbies etc., for there will always be lessons to be learnt in every aspect.

Just because I'm writing a book doesn't make me perfect, and just because I'm not perfect doesn't mean I shouldn't write a book. I'm in a continuous process of learning, erring, researching, growing, slipping up, developing, and whatever I'm putting down on paper is only on the basis of my current understanding of that subject. It's important to me that I release it, get it published, and then have a clearer mind, so that I'm able to make way for more new insights to occur. It's like if a mobile phone manufacturer only did R&D over R&D, and not put out their current model, then they would be waiting forever. Instead, what they do is release their latest model and go back to doing more R&D for their future models. Exploration is an ongoing and never-ending process, just like the concept of *kaizen*.

Everything that is being said here has already been said at some point or another in some way or another by someone or another – like a visionary leader, philosopher, spiritual guru or a personal development teacher. I'm not saying that I am like any one of the above, but these things have always been said since time immemorial.

The core of this work, to put it simply, is acknowledging and understanding the ego. Any identification or labelling, and any separation or prejudice – whether that's with your body, your family, your country or your likes and dislikes – is all ego. Let's first appreciate that it's impossible to live without the ego – even doing basic things like brushing teeth, bathing and eating is done because of ego. The more we become aware of its presence and its necessity, the less we can let it run our life.

By doing spiritual work, introspection and self-enquiry, one is able to become less ego-centric and find their own balance between the two extremities of selfishness and selflessness, knowing well that the self or ego lies in both.

P.S. There's no *i* in selflessness and wellness, only in selfishness and illness.

Many of you may put down this book because of the innumerable contradictions in it. And since almost everyone has very strong beliefs and perspectives about several aspects, such as religion, atheism, science, food, family, career etc., everything has to conveniently and comfortably fit into those perspectives and be black and white. So, unless you're able to move away from being rigid and inflexible, it may be quite easy for you to move away from this book.

This book is not like a quick-fix motivational presentation. I'm not here to entertain, amuse or talk about things that will inspire and motivate you. I'm not here to make friends, and don't mind if you were to totally reject my thoughts and ideas. In fact, some of the things I say may cause disturbance within you. I am also not here to teach anything or offer a panacea, but to be able to learn along with you some of the things that we can do to elevate our everyday existence.

I'm as much a student of life as you are, trying to educate myself, and to understand what this thing called life is. What I'd like to share with you here are some ideas and concepts which, if not necessarily fully applied but even merely understood, can help us lead lives that may be worthwhile. The intention is not to thrust these upon you or force you into accepting them. Just as a gold trader checks gold before buying, you too are free to examine the ideas I share. However, as you're reading, I ask that you "empty your cup" and keep an open mind.

I do not ascribe to any religion and none of the things I say will be with the intention of proselytising you to any faith. The whole idea behind this book is to share ideas that I've learnt and continue to learn in this journey of the Self, one that has completely turned my life around. And I plan to spend the rest of my life "evangelising" about it, as religious as that may sound.

"Why should I empty my cup?"

Well, that is a choice you have. But if you really want to live an inspired and meaningful life, then open-mindedness, inclusiveness and flexibility have to be of high importance to you. This means that you need to always keep a clean slate, and let yourself be guided by everything that comes your way i.e. not fight or complain about them. When you're full of conclusions and absolutes then nothing more can be absorbed or grasped. With a "beginner's mind", you can live and function from the perspective of being a humble student of life – learning to always trust that everything coming into your life is teaching and guiding you, and is in alignment with your vision and purpose.

Today is the first day of the rest of your life, and investing in cultivating your wisdom is the best investment you will ever make. Ever! It will not only improve your life, but also the lives of those around you. And it all starts by first emptying your own cup.

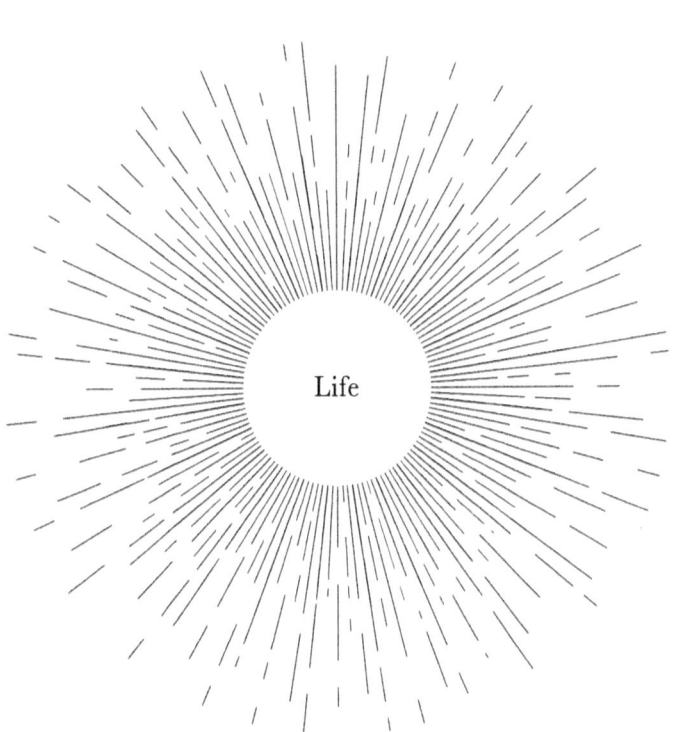

There's only you. There's nobody else in your world other than you. Understand this! Please!! You don't have to do anything for anyone. Just look after yourself, and take the best care of whatever you think constitutes you. If you think you're the body and the mind, then just care for and look after these two aspects of you. I don't want to give you any suggestions or tips on how to look after them – figure out for yourself what you think is good for your body and mind and make it a practice. Whatever that may be.

We think our mind is on auto-pilot and that we don't have any control over it. Actually, the one thing, the only thing we have complete control over is our mind.

Life is all about learning, growing and developing, but there are impediments, almost all of them within you, that will not allow you to prosper. One of the biggest ones is that 4-letter word that starts with F. The more we Fear, the more risk-averse we become, which then impedes our growth even more. Did you know there are many who even fear success?

Another impediment or barrier to growth and development is being intellectually closed – reading and journaling are two of the best ways to combat this, and to keep you from closing. When you're listening to some wisdom on a podcast or on the web, do not discount the value it's providing you. Even if you don't apply any of the wisdom immediately, at least be open to the ideas and suggestions.

Your body and mind are a consequence of your *karma*; your environment, experiences and your responses to them.

Things happen, and they're just situations, metaphors and figures of speech. Everything that's happening around you are only circumstances. They're only situations that happen, and you just happen to be at the centre of it all. And because you have senses, particularly the sense of sight, touch and hearing, you unknowingly judge the people around those situations.

Try for a moment to judge and language a situation. Then attempt to remove all the labels, the people, the words and the meaning attached to it. What's left? *You* experiencing the situation, and responding to it.

I believe that actualisation and self-development (which we're all constantly working on, mostly unconsciously) are the only things to pursue. And one of the key areas to develop is our mental and emotional well-being.

We're all emotionally driven, and how we feel is more important than anything else. As we work on having our emotions under control, every area of our life will start to align with that inner feeling – whether that's in the aspect of health, career, relationships or even finance. All of these external factors are only reflections of our inner self, most of all how we feel about those aspects.

We live in a society where most people are heavily invested in denial. In a way, even some of the traditional personal development and spiritual teachings propagate this dogmatic way of living. In our quest to be "positive" all the time we've lost what it really means to be human. I come across people every now and then who are just products of this positive thinking movement and spend their energy stuffing and denying their feelings in the pursuit of "being positive". Being truly positive is to positively *experience* the full – yes, the entire range of human emotions including the "negative" ones. You don't necessarily always have to take actions based on those negative emotions. True positive thinking is being inclusive and accepting of whatever is happening. It is what it is – regardless of whether the happening is "good" for you or not. Unfortunately, this kind of thinking is very uncommon, and it's all because of a poor relationship one has with one's own self.

Being stuck in the "false positive" mode actually shuts off your creative abilities and disallows you from experiencing your full potential. Creativity is your natural state, and feeling your full range of emotions unleashes that creativity even more. Of course, at times it may seem easier to just stuff it and slap on a smiley face. But remember, it will come back to haunt you. Anything that is suppressed can express itself in later days and uglier ways. There is no value in lying to yourself; if you want to reach your true self, you must have a strong foundation, grounded in a relationship with yourself. If you don't enjoy spending time alone then you must not be in very good company.

You are your own guru. Your guru is not outside of you, rather within. Think about it, who is the one that surrenders oneself to someone else? You do. It's your own intention to make someone a guru. Because you sense something about the other person, that you believe they have and you don't. Remember, you see others only as you are. You don't have to follow or become a disciple of any person or demigod other than yourself.

The Sanskrit word *guru* is defined as *one who dispels darkness*. *Gu* means *darkness* or *ignorance* and *Ru* means *dispeller*. No matter how much the teacher teaches you, it is your intention and open-mindedness, and your own ability to grasp the teaching that determines the learning and understanding. If you are not interested, focussed, keen, curious and excited to listen, observe and learn, no matter how much effort the teacher puts in, it may not bear any fruit. And bear in mind, there's only learning – even when the teacher is teaching, the main thing that is happening is learning, even for the teacher.

Another definition of the word guru is "one who is beyond attributes and forms". Which is again you. The real *you*, the intangible You. Not the body you, but the one that governs the body – the life, the spirit, the soul. One that's beyond all attributes and forms – none other than the supreme Self. One that resides within each one of us. One who understands truth, is seeking truth, and is open to the whole idea of truth is the real guru. Those who provide the education are teachers or preceptors. They happen to be the one communicating the message and meaning using words, language, or even actions and body language. A teacher who teaches others has had a teacher themselves. The one who has no guru above oneself is the true guru, and that is you.

We're not human doings, we're human beings. There's nothing that we have to do, only be. Be curious, be flexible, be open-minded, be aware, be conscious, be inclusive. Everything is experience, there's only experience. And who's the one experiencing everything? You, me, each one of us! All this experiencing is done through our senses and with our minds.

One of the important factors about non-duality is that this very thing we call life, soul or consciousness cannot do anything without the body, and vice versa. Life cannot be experienced unless it's in a body, and the body cannot function unless there's life in it. Life and body are two but one, it's almost like saying $1+1=1$

You will start to question beliefs and ideologies in a big way as you expand your sphere of understanding and knowledge, and become more aware. You'll become skeptical about ideals and doctrines that not only the world holds, but even that you hold. And just because a majority, in fact almost all of humanity, hold similar beliefs about education, career, work, family, adventure, religion or science, doesn't necessarily mean they're all correct – for no belief is equal to truth. A belief is in no way inclusive or conscious, it's rather quite the opposite. The worst part is most ideological people are clueless that the "moral" and "rational" ideas they so tightly hold on to are just beliefs.

Ask yourself the following question,
and try answering it without using any words or labels:

"What am I?"

Your level of success will rarely exceed your level of personal development, because success is something you manifest by the person you become. You really need to think of yourself as someone who's continuously developing and growing; therefore, you cannot measure yourself by who you are today, but rather who you are becoming by what you're consistently doing. How you are as a person within determines how you are without. Your "external" life cannot be any bigger than your "internal".

Balance doesn't mean finding the exact central point between any two extremities. The idea is to be fluid and flexible, as if you're walking a tightrope or riding a bike. It's about not being too rigid, yet not being too casual or skeptical. Likewise, the true self lies somewhere between the two extremities of selfishness and selflessness, and it depends where your point of balance is. Each of us has a different point: some may have to lean more towards the selfish side to achieve the right balance, and some towards the selfless.

An awakening experience is when you have a sudden surge of clarity about reality and truth, when your awareness expands and intensifies, when your perceptions of the world around you become more clear, and you transcend the worries that normally preoccupy you. That being said, most of us spend our entire lives in denial, chasing things, or just being busy on our devices. And we experience or understand the concept of awakening only on our deathbeds, maybe moments before we take our last breath. How sad is that?!

At the very core, each of us is actually beyond all biases and prejudices, however our deep-rooted and stubborn conditioning doesn't allow us to touch that infinite dimension. Hence we're unable to perceive anyone or anything from that non-dual perspective. Each one of us, at our very essence, is infinite intelligence, or god, devoid of any identity or division. You are god – as dualistic a sentence that is. Even though I've somehow articulated that, please consider that language is nonetheless binary and dualistic. It's impossible to explain non-duality using a dualistic tool like language. Therefore in that context, sentences such as I am god, you are god, he/she is god are all baseless.

While we're on the subject of grammar, let's conjugate the verb "to be" in the present tense and compose a sentence with a subject and predicate. Now, the moment you place the conjugated "be" after a pronoun or a name (subject) you have created an identity. And if you add another word after that, you have created a sentence that has an identity and a separation (predicate). However, what I'm referring to here as god, is one without an identity or division, as in only a pronoun or name by itself – as one complete sentence, not merely as a word. Again, the word I, or you, or he, or she as a sentence, is what I'm referring to as god – and this completely contradicts language, but that's probably the best way I could define god with words. There's only god, there's only consciousness, there's only you.

It's not about reading about it
It's not about being told about it
It's not about learning about it
It's not about knowing about it
It's not about knowing it
It's not about understanding it
It's not about getting it
It's not about really getting it
It's not about really really getting it
It's not about making it a part of you
It's not about embodying it
It's not about you living it
It's not about you becoming it and it becoming you
It has to be you and you it, that's it.
For it is you and you it.

Thoughts and emotions are physical in nature. That's right, they always have a physiological effect in the body, although we may take them to be mental and intangible.

Why I say they're physical is because every thought or feeling has to manifest itself somehow somewhere – like cause and effect – and the only place it can first evince is the very physiology it has occurred in. Read that line again. Effects of placebo and nocebo are perfect examples. Prior to releasing any new medication, placebo trials are always conducted to rule out the possibility of the mind having played any part in the healing process. I'm not saying that the mind is the only factor, but it is an important one, that cannot and should not be ignored. It's like if I asked you to merely imagine squeezing the sour juices of a lemon into your mouth, your mouth will start to salivate. Another obvious example is of getting aroused, if you were to merely think of carnal thoughts they automatically have an effect on your body parts.

Important: have you noticed that any negative thoughts or feelings you have – like anger, stress, sadness, fear, guilt, anxiety, shame, nervousness – show in your body immediately, in the form of palpitations, sweaty palms, shortness of breath or faster heartbeat? However, positive thoughts and feelings don't so much. Why? Because your body's natural state of homeostasis is of ease, wellness, bliss and peace. Think about that one.

When you're in a mode of *vichara* or enquiry, it's all about questions, not so much about the answers. There's no "one answer" anyway, that will take your life towards permanent joy and bliss, actualisation or enlightenment. The fact that this journey in itself is called "self-enquiry" is fascinating. You're only enquiring. Even words like contemplation and introspection are all about questioning, not about solutions or answers. We're so conditioned to be fixated on finding answers that we avoid being fully curious, and in the process, miss experiencing life to the fullest. A full life is one that has more, varied and interesting experiences in it, and being curious plays a big part in creating that.

So these questions don't necessarily need to be formulated in a particular manner or even in any language, as long as the curiosity comes through. Even just being in a state of awe and wonder has an underlying basis of inquisitiveness to it.

As for me, my *questions* are becoming clearer as I evolve, and I have a better understanding of them and where they're leading me.

We don't see anything as it is. We only see it as we are, through our own set of lenses, perspectives and paradigms. Even the trivial everyday situations and circumstances that we're confronted with are all reflections of our inner self, broadly speaking, of our psychology and our philosophy.

Your age, or the length of your life so far, has nothing to do with it. No matter how young or old you are, the moment you see even the slightest opening of that figurative door to the Self, your life will start to become euphoric. You can't help but let that awareness take over your life and allow it to guide you all the time. Maybe for the first time in your life you'll start to properly notice and observe the profundity of everything. Not only will your sense of comprehension and understanding of everything become more intense, but even your sense of faith, courage and joy will become so profound that it'll bring tears to your eyes.

A lot of older people believe that they have a whole experience of life behind them – "I've been around, I've seen a lot" types, and tend to quantify everything. However, it's really not about how long you live, but how you live. It's the quality of life that matters most, which is directly dependent on how present you are to experience the profundity of it. How deep and wide you've explored life is what constitutes a full life.

You are life, can you believe that? Why can't you comprehend that?

Self-enquiry or introspection is not like a meditation session that you only do at particular times – you do it throughout your waking hours, irrespective of what you're doing. There's no difference between working or playing and doing self-enquiry, and with a little practice it can be done under any circumstance. And please, you don't have to give up your job, family, business, hobbies or your social life to do self-enquiry. As for me, when I first started doing it, it was mostly during the wee hours of the morning, which in no time turned into a 24/7 obsession, even in sleep. There wasn't anything else I could think, discuss or talk about for at least the first few years.

When opportunity knocks on your door you have to be fully ready to open the door immediately, for if you delay opening the door, opportunity will grow impatient and leave your door to go knocking on other doors.

If you haven't heard or read about Spiral Dynamics, I urge you to look it up. It's a model that was developed to describe consciousness and awareness – both at an individual level and collective, such as societies and organisations. Spiral Dynamics describes eight levels, expressed in value systems each with their own colours. These levels climb from simple structure to increasing complexity. What I'm trying to do here is to discuss this model from a consciousness perspective.

Every level or stage has to be fully included even if not directly experienced. Each stage has to be incorporated into one's very being. You don't need to behave or act upon every stage but it has to be mentally, psychologically, emotionally and spiritually comprehended and sustained. Every little nuance of each stage has to be understood as if you are in that situation. It's not about going up the stages but it's more like a circle, and expansion is the key, which is what open-mindedness and inclusiveness is all about.

Everything I'm doing or saying is in no way better, more evolved or conscious than anything or anyone. Some may think so, not me. It just happens to be my thing. Just as you'd prefer one thing over another, my personal interest lies in enquiry, contemplation and philosophy. For instance, you probably place your career over contemplating the nature of reality – with me it's just the other way around. You may consider family more important than introspecting about the Self, I don't necessarily. Making money is probably at the top of your priorities, it isn't on mine. And all this is in no way profound or wise-talk. I'm not trying to be humble, nor am I belittling myself. I wouldn't consider this kind of talk by anyone to be sagacious or shrewd; this just happens to be a hobby of mine, it's just my thing.

When you look at the theory of evolution, it has been written and formulated from a human point of view – that it took millions of years for Earth to form, and thousands of years before water hit Earth. It then took another thousands of years for the first living creatures to emanate out of water onto land, and how the four-legged animal became a two-legged human. These are theories, speculations and hypotheses. How can we take them to be valid or True with a capital T? This here, right now – the present moment is all that is True. The *only* reality.

Most people seem to have quite a clear understanding of right and wrong, and good and bad. Even I used to, well kind of. But now I like to enquire and explore different possibilities, and view things from a "relativity" viewpoint.

Let's try and define good and bad. Anything that is efficient, useful, healthy and sustainable is considered good, and that that isn't isn't. I'm thinking, aren't the wrong just products of the right, and vice-versa? Aren't they more complementary than contradictory? Can there be one without the other? So then why are we always trying to be correct and right? I've noticed people tend to be quite stuck up about morality and ethics. If they see something that is not "right", they moan about it or do everything to legislate and rectify it to whatever they think is right. Or if they're slightly democratic they will get the consent of "the people" and go with what the majority considers appropriate.

My question is, how do we decide what is right and what's not? We all know of concepts and theories that were once wrong but are now right. And the other way around. So isn't right and wrong only two sides of the same coin? Isn't this concept of right vs wrong and good vs bad more subjective, than objective?

Yoga is more so what you do off the mat, than what you do on it. The definition that Yoga is twisting and turning your body, doing various strange postures, breathing exercises and meditation is not entirely complete, as these are only some aspects of yoga. *Yoga*, a Sanskrit word translated as *union*, is the conscious practising of how one functions psychologically and physiologically whilst being connected with all life.

It's basically how aware and conscious you are as an individual, how you speak, how you carry yourself, your ability to pay attention to everything and the intention behind everything you do. It's also about how you interact with not only people, but with everything, including your pets, others' pets, the entire animal life, and even inanimate objects. How you treat not just the plants in your garden, but all trees and plants everywhere. How you treat all people as yourself, and as your own family and friends.

So yoga is an entire collection of spiritual practices and techniques that includes and emphasises different approaches, and ultimately leads to the ongoing goal of awakening, unification, liberation and enlightenment.

You only see what they want you to see. No matter what is happening in your city or state or the world, the news media will show you what they want you to see – what generates excitement, sensation and to a degree, fear. And we call that News. I'm not blaming the media alone here. As much as it is their responsibility to bring to you what's most important and relevant (which they're probably doing to a degree), what can they do when almost the entire population gets titillated by low conscious hogwash and is craving for it more and more?

I don't know if true journalism even exists today, it's all gone yellow. If reality TV has become today's thing, then what more can I say?! Same goes with advertising, it's no longer interesting or intelligent – almost all commercials reek of phoney morality, and is filled with disclaimers. In the commercials, the companies portray themselves as kind and caring, but when you actually visit the businesses, their customer service is close to appalling.

It'll take a few lifetimes or generations before we can start to see a positive change in the media, and this can happen only when there's an authentic development in consciousness, at both an individual and collective level. And well, we have to truly want it first.

A lot of people get the big realisation about life when they're on their deathbed, and live their last few days with regret. But after all, who isn't dying? This is not a philosophical question. We are mortals, mere mortals, but when you look at the way most people go about their daily lives, one gets the impression that they are immortal. I consider myself to be on my "deathbed" right now, and I don't want to live with any regrets anymore, least of all the regret of not understanding or discussing the most important things in and about life.

This book that I'm writing is, in a small way, to help you look at life with wide open eyes and a broader perspective, and transcend any conditioning. We all have it within us to follow the path of enquiry – to question what reality is, what the self is and what consciousness is. Like I said, on the previous page, we have to truly want it first.

You can listen to all the personal development teachers, follow all the gurus and mystics, read all the religious and holy books, even be a spiritual teacher yourself, but it's not good enough – until you fully embody all the teachings yourself, live them and breathe them.

Reading, listening to and watching videos may get you motivated, but if all you do is intellectualise and philosophise about all that, at some point it'll start to make you feel sorry and sad for yourself. So stop following, and just start being all that. Is it easy? Hell, no! It's easier said than done.

Not everything I say will resonate with everyone every time. There'll be things that may resonate with one, but not with another. In fact, there will be things that may resonate with you today but not tomorrow, or something that did not resonate with you yesterday may today. We're all different people. So if you understand this or resonate with this, then, like it or not, you're a spiritual person. Taking the spiritual path means that you're open, fluid, flexible and inclusive – not just in the present moment, but also in regards to the past and future.

Having a different breakfast every morning is one of the best practices I adopted a few years ago. Be it toast, *upma*, eggs, *parathas*, smoothie, waffles, pancakes, oats, muesli or something else – a different breakfast every day is what makes each day so exciting and refreshing. Even skip it once every few days.

As much as it's important to have a routine, it's equally important to not have one. It's okay to mix things up. Be brave, adventurous and explore possibilities. Flexibility is a great virtue. When we're rigid, cling to one position and are not willing to let our hearts be moved a little by different ideas, then we can easily be broken. Instead, let's be intentionally variable, and try a different breakfast every morning.

I've heard that there are people who don't believe in morals – not really nihilists, but these are people who've transcended the dualities of good and bad, and right and wrong. They neither believe in science nor religion, or even spirituality. These people just *are*.

There are few who are aware they're aware, there are those who are aware they're not aware, but then there are those who aren't even aware they aren't aware.

Feeling, although an emotion, is in a sense the sense of touch. This sentence pretty much corroborates the fact that feelings are physical in nature, something that we do with our entire body – not just with our hands and feet. Our skin is our largest organ and the sense of touch is one of the five senses. So, when you – the *inner* you – get angry, the anger starts at the metaphysical level, and after travelling through your entire anatomy, makes it all the way to the most exterior part of your physiology i.e. the skin, hence the expression "red with anger". Similarly, your skin is constantly absorbing the environment and sending messages to the innermost part of you, to the real you. Thus, you can see that there's a constant perforated transaction happening between the physical you and the metaphysical you.

Being cool, chilled, carefree or *bindaas* is one of the most desired or wonderful states of being – it's almost like an enlightened state. I'm sure we've all met people who are really cool, even you must've been in that state at some point. There's something about these James Bond-esque kinds of people – they never seem to get shaken or stirred by anything. And it's not their clothes, looks, physique or money that makes them cool. They're an entirely different package. At the very core of their being is *less*, as in minimal. Think about that one. They're not fidgety, don't speak unnecessarily, they're confident but not arrogant, they're not needy or desperate, they're authentic and open to self-disclosure, they're witty, good conversationalists aka good listeners, and physiology-wise they practise good health and hygiene. Importantly, they don't only act cool when they're around family or friends, but that's just how they always are, even when no one's watching.

If you're struggling to achieve a career or health goal, it's only because you haven't changed – the only way you can achieve it is by actually taking on a new personality. It's ridiculous to anticipate a new outcome when you're still following your old patterns and routines, and you're still your former self.

Einstein said that insanity is doing the same thing over and over again and expecting different results. Your "external" life is only a reflection of your "internal", so change has to first happen within.

A few years ago when I "didn't" get a parking ticket, I celebrated it. I had parked my car in a 1 hour parking spot and didn't return to my car until after about 2 hours, and to my surprise there was no ticket! I got pretty excited by the potential money saved, and took the girls out for a nice meal. I still do this – not that I'm always parking illegally – but every time I believe I've saved money, I celebrate by spending it. However, now that I've spent some time in self-enquiry and introspection, I have a much deeper understanding of what gratitude means, and all the reasons to be thankful. Come to think of it, I'm always saving money when I don't fall sick, every time fuel prices don't go up, or when I don't miss a flight. What I'm trying to impart here is to be open to living each day counting blessings and being grateful, humbly remembering – no matter what, it could be worse.

If you were to look at some of the popular psychological models and theories like Abraham Maslow's *Hierarchy of Needs*, Dr David Hawkins' *Map of Consciousness*, Clare Graves' *Spiral Dynamics*, or Cook-Greuter's *Ego Development*, you'll see that the main aspect is the vertical (and a bit horizontal) development of the human psyche – individual and collective. However, we first need to understand that these are only maps that have been created to simplify highly intricate concepts like reality and consciousness using a straightforward linear design. The map is not the territory.

To understand reality, the self or consciousness, one doesn't need to go up the different stages/levels, with the ultimate goal or vision to reach the topmost stage or to even transcend it. True understanding of reality, self and consciousness happens only when one is fully inclusive and accepting of all stages from a *being* position, as in how they truly are at their essence. Otherwise it just becomes a game of morals – to become morally spiritual or spiritually moral. To articulate it as best as I can, it's about separating and detaching oneself from each stage yet fully including them. Each and every stage of those models has to be entirely included, and built upon. Somewhat like how we go through education – we don't ignore the learning from primary and secondary school when we go to university. One needs to totally accept and include the positives and also the negatives of each stage. I'm not saying that you need to then become, behave or act *according* to that stage, but rather wholly *include* every aspect of that stage into your very own self, at *being* level.

All of us are on a certain level of awareness and consciousness, which can be defined as an understanding of reality, and/or our ability to perceive reality. Our perception of reality is based on the environment we're born and raised in, our experiences, and our responses to the experiences. Our environment and understanding of reality is affected and programmed by parents, siblings, teachers, friends, people, media, language, labels and more. And as we grow up and begin to experience independence and freedom in a small way, we start to even program ourselves. Not all of this programming happens as a result of our own choice. At lower levels of consciousness, we don't even believe we have a choice in what we believe, and constantly blame circumstances or people for all that we are.

Heightening, elevating or raising consciousness is about enhancing our perceptions through direct experience, self-enquiry, introspection and exploration, starting from a point of detachment, radical open-mindedness, humility and infinite flexibility. It is not based on beliefs or conditioning – it's beyond everything, even concepts of birth and death, and also beyond the experiencing of life itself.

Can you resolve this? "Yes". Then why worry?

Can you resolve this? "No". Then why worry?

Worrying is *thinking* about what you don't want, but what can get you out of worrying is *thinking* itself. Counterintuitive, right?! Let's break it down. The first kind of thinking is subjective and the second objective. The former has feelings and emotions in it, the latter introspection and contemplation. As much as feelings are an inherent part of us and pretty much run our lives, we can through objective thinking not let them get the better of us – simply by stepping back from our usual train of thought and examining it critically and thoroughly.

"How could you say that?!" Many relationships hinge on the base foundations of language – what one *says* to another is deemed more important than how they *are*. All it takes is one line, a sentence or even a mere word that can end long-standing relationships – and all the positive aspects of the past are completely disregarded in an instant.

The importance of creativity in your life. I cannot stress enough that each one of us is creative in some way, not figuratively speaking but literally – we're all artists! Creativity doesn't mean you have to do art, music, film, poetry, dance or photography. Anything can be done from a creative angle. It's not what you do but how, and that's where creativity comes in. Finding new ways of doing old things can also be considered as being creative. I don't mean that you now need to change systems. You can very well keep doing the same things in the same manner, but while you're doing, please be open to your intuitions which may suggest a different approach. And try it out – if it works, good; if it doesn't, at least you can rule it out.

Remove negativity from your life! Easier said than done. Your negative expressions, words, behaviours and emotions manifest in your experiences and in your body – in the form of pain, discomfort, sickness or disease, while the positive ones don't. Why? Because homeostasis, equilibrium and equanimity happen to be the default, the norm. Removing negative thoughts may be the most challenging – that's why it's better to take the back door i.e. by having positive feelings, adopting positive behaviours and using positive language.

Equanimity, like flexibility and detachment, is a mental attitude and has nothing to do with someone or something outside of yourself, it's all within – just like peace and joy have always been with you, within, and will continue to be with you, within.

Being inclusive doesn't mean you have to now start hoarding stuff. You have to most importantly include minimalism into your life.

Have less, be more. Minimalism isn't just about getting rid of all your stuff and living with barely anything. It is in fact a mindset – of having fewer things, doing fewer things, and being fewer things, as opposed to having, doing and being all things.

Have you ever thought about doing away with cable TV or even regular TV? We gave them up many years ago, and love the fact that we don't watch commercials or have the TV on all day. Advertisements are one of the biggest enemies of minimalism, so reducing or eliminating exposure to low-conscious commercials is a game changer. Minimalism is also about quality over quantity – always buy the best. Furthermore, note that minimalism isn't about "outta sight outta mind" – you also need to evaluate things that are tucked away in closets, drawers and cupboards.

Consider for just a moment how different your life would look if you owned fewer things, like clothes and shoes; you'd have more disposable income, and more time to live your life – mornings would be less stressful, your closets would be well-organised and uncluttered, packing for trips would take less time, laundry would be easier. As you can see, there are a lot of advantages in having a minimalist lifestyle.

What we currently are is the result of our future. Does that sentence even make sense?! Is the current state of your health, your career, the level of abundance in your life, the quality of your relationships really the consequence of the... future?! Not at all, it's the result of your past! All that we are right now is the result of our past thoughts, choices, actions, environment and experiences. So if your present is the result of your past, it also means that you're creating your future through your present experiences, thoughts, actions, and choices. And depending on how good a visionary you are, or how goal-oriented you are, you can keep creating your future in the present. So, you can see how important it is to be a visionary and have clear and well-defined goals. Most people don't even have goals, forget about written ones. What's your BHAG?!

Neglect is like an infection. Left unchecked it will spread throughout our entire system of disciplines and eventually lead to a complete breakdown of a potentially joy-filled and prosperous life. Neglecting to do the things we know we should be doing causes us to feel guilty, and guilt leads to an erosion of self-confidence. As our self-confidence diminishes, so does the level of our activity. And as our activity diminishes, our results decline. And as our results suffer, our attitude begins to weaken. And as our attitude shifts, our self-confidence diminishes even more… and on and on it goes.

So go ahead and set goals that will change your life, read books that will affect your thinking and your ideas, go to seminars and lectures, and be around other happy and successful people. Faith and fear cannot coexist – you have to let go of one, preferably the latter.

If you're unhappy that you're unhappy and happy that you're happy, then that's a problem.

If making money makes you happy and losing sad, then that's an issue.

If you only want good health and no sickness, then you're in trouble.

If you only want positive emotions and no negative ones, then that's a worry.

If you only want the good and no bad at all, then it's time to change that perspective.

What I'm alluding to here is about resisting, and what you resist persists. If you resist one but not the other, then that's a concern. A full, abundant and complete life is one that is all-inclusive, without any kind of biases – one that always stays open to everything, attached to nothing, and never closes.

What the COVID-19 pandemic has taught us is to look after our individual self well. That's it. Any virus can exist only if there's a host. When Mother Teresa said that if each of us would only sweep our own doorstep, the whole world would be clean, she meant to just take full responsibility for yourself. The least you can do is to look after your health and physiology, whether that's through diet and fasting, rest and recreation, or fitness and exercise. Or all of the above.

If we took away all labels, even the fact that we're "human beings", then the only commonality among all of us is that we're living. And obviously the only other commonality is that we exist in a tactile and tangible body. We took birth in a body and so will we take death too. As the body started functioning with our birth so will it stop with our death.

We are all in a physical object called body, and life is happening within this body and with the help of the body. Although there's only infinite consciousness or eternal life, any living being can only exist in a body. Therefore, without a physical body there cannot be a living being, and vice versa. However, consciousness is the only thing that doesn't have a beginning or an end, and is all around – not just among people but in animals, birds, insects, plants, trees, sea creatures and even in inanimate objects, it's everywhere.

If you have a problem with your partner, child, sibling, parent, friend, or colleague, you can and should only discuss it with your partner, child, sibling, parent, friend, or colleague, respectively. The key word in that line is "respectively", otherwise it'll be called gossip, talking behind one's back or even slander.

About tennis and full self-expression:

A top-ranked tennis player like fill-in-the-blank is one who expresses themself fully. It doesn't really matter whom they're playing against. They don't necessarily even compete against their opponent. They just do everything to express their fullest potential, whether that be moving around the court, conserving energy, racket positioning, chasing balls, hitting them or taking risks and going for the lines. This can only be achieved when the mind and body (thoughts and actions) are in alignment and the player expresses themself fully, sans any restrictions. Technically speaking, to win a men's grand slam tournament, he has to win 7 matches in a row, which means 21 sets or at least 126 games or at least 504 points. And to lift that trophy, the majority of the points, at least the crucial or defining ones, have to be played with intent, focus, and devotion, all of which are elements of full self-expression.

As you do one thing, so you do another. I know most of you would immediately disagree and say something like: "I can never cook the way I work". Please hear me out. Gandhi said that life is one indivisible whole, and as much as it was primarily meant from a holonic perspective, it was also said from a very yogic or spiritual perspective. What he meant was that the intention, devotion, attitude and care you put in to doing one thing cannot change when you're doing something else, because they are all qualities of the inherent you, which cannot be separated from any activity that you're doing, whatever that may be.

Even the fact that you completely stay away from doing certain things is, if not out of fear, because of the subconscious or conscious awareness of your own self – for you know that if you did do that thing, you couldn't do it without putting your entire personality and attitude into it.

What does it take to become open-minded and inclusive?
1. Cultivating an attitude of curiosity
2. Becoming eager to widen your perspectives
3. Broadening your knowledge.
4. Adopting skepticism, as in philosophical skepticism.
5. Not being conclusive, or an absolutist.
6. Not holding on to anything too tightly.
7. Questioning everything, even (especially) the most obvious things.

Dogma and ideologies are not reserved for religious people only. Not at all! Almost everyone is in one way or another dogmatic and ideological including most intellectuals, atheists, sceptics, scientific people and nihilists, to name just a few.

"I can't eat that, I don't drink that, I'm not a winter person, I don't watch those kinds of films, I hate going to the city, I just can't go out without makeup, I can't do a call centre job, I'm not a cat person, I can't bear people smoking, it's not my kind of music", and the list goes on and on and on. We all have two kinds of lists. In this piece, I won't be talking about the "willing" list but the other kind – that list of things we're unwilling to be, do or have.

We build our entire lives around that "unwilling" list. Sadly it becomes our very identity. And the more things we have on that list, the more constricted and cramped our life becomes. Most people have more things on the unwilling list, than on the willing. That shows how rigid and inflexible they are. There's nothing wrong in having a "willing to be, do, have" list, which can be as long as possible, but what I'm stressing here is to think about the unwilling one. Is it possible to live without having anything on this list? Probably not. It's not possible to have a blank list, but the fewer things we have on it, the more unbound, free and independent we can live our lives, and with lesser resistance.

It's alright, it's okay. All things must pass, and this too shall pass – whether it's a challenging situation or a pleasant one. The coming and going of highs and lows, ups and downs, and happiness and unhappiness are like the seasons. They are dynamic, and in constant flux that come and go. The wise learn to tolerate both without being disturbed. Yes, happiness can be as disturbing as unhappiness.

Having faith and trust is about being detached, and it means that no matter what comes into your life, positive or negative, will most certainly pass and you will get over it. *When* is the only question. Not to mention that even the passing away passes away, leaving behind an ongoing and continuous passing away.
Fana al fana.

I asked: "how many of you have dunked a cookie, biscuit or doughnut into a hot beverage and it has broken into the drink?" Almost all hands went up. I then asked: "how many of you got over it?" Almost all hands went up.

That's just how the cookie crumbles. Take this metaphor and apply it to all events and happenings (negative or positive) in your life.

I took up my first job in 1988 as a telex operator in the communications department of Pan American Airways in New Delhi, and since then I've worked in different industries doing different roles in cities of Mumbai, Auckland and Melbourne. The jobs include: airline security officer, flight attendant, *carnatic* music teacher, campervan rental supervisor, banker, advertising executive, copywriter, call centre agent, health insurance agent, kinesiologist, complaints resolution specialist, life coach, retail assistant, roadside assistance agent, cafe kitchen hand, barista, rideshare driver, and administrator.

The only purpose in life is to fully awaken and actualise, and we keep getting messages and opportunities from everywhere to slowly make our way towards that coveted place. Which is why personal development teachers, sages, spiritual masters, yogis and mystics come on our path, to help us stay focussed on that mission, and to expedite the process.

Our body is a responding machine. Besides doing several other things – many of which science hasn't been able to find answers to – the body is constantly responding to our innermost sense of being, be it feelings and thoughts on a fundamental level or beliefs and conditioning from a deeper understanding. Whether you call the response illness, wellness or give it a medical name, it's just a response or reflection of your inner state.

What I've discovered in my years of experimentation with self-healing is the concept of wait and watch. I try not to act in haste, or interfere with what the body is doing. We've all learnt about our body's own immune system which is there to protect the body from harmful substances, germs and foreign organisms. And as long as our immune system is running smoothly, we don't even notice that it's there. But if it stops working properly – because it's weak or can't fight aggressive germs – we get ill. What I've found is that the more things we have on that "list of things we are unwilling to be, do or have", the harder the body will have to work in order to create homeostasis.

One of the more apparent ways to allow the body to be at ease (not dis-ease) is by not overloading or feeding the mind with thoughts and feelings of worry and anxiety. If you've heard of placebo, then look up nocebo. I'm not saying medicine and treatments are unimportant. All I'm saying is that our beliefs, thoughts and feelings have the ability to create sickness as much as it can create wellness, and we need to be open to exploring this dimension too.

"I take a lot of pride in my work". I hear this line a lot. You don't need to say anything or take pride in your work, you only need to do your work. People are so particular about saying the right things, or being nice and polite that they don't realise that the best way to be kind to someone is by just doing what needs to be done, especially if you're in the service industry. (Well, who isn't in the service industry?!)

Being kind or nice is only the icing on the cake. Just do what you say. As a matter of fact you don't even need to say it, just do what you're supposed to do.

Every now and then I get to a point where I start to bottle up, and become very hesitant to speak up and express what I think and feel. I'm realising that much of the hesitation is due to the challenge of being able to articulate many of my thoughts and intuitions effectively.

Language is only a medium that we use to communicate the ideas and intuitions we get. Even if we mastered a language, we can still only express and explain the ideas within the confines of that language. We don't necessarily think in any language, we just think. But the only tool we have to articulate those thoughts is language, which has its own boundaries and limitations.

How could reality ever be *fully* expressed with language when it can only be experienced? You can experience the taste of truth, but how can you fully express that taste with language?

Consciousness is the intention that allows a seed to sprout, moves a thought across our minds, grows grass and our fingernails, and keeps everything in motion – all at the same time. There's only consciousness – what we are, where we are, everything we sense is all consciousness.

What's important to understand is that we have the power within ourselves to connect to that source consciously while we're still living in it – by simply paying attention to the life that we are. Just to the very *life* – no mind, no body, no stories, no words, no labels or language.

Sometimes I wonder what kind of conversations I should have with people. What can I talk about – weather, politics, work, news, money, sport? Been there done that, almost my entire life, and it's only now that I've chosen to deliberate and focus on something else. Never in the past have I been so obsessed with introspecting the self, deconstructing reality or contemplating consciousness, all of which have now become more important to me than anything else. And even if I did engage in discussing any of the aforementioned topics, I would now do it from the point of view of consciousness or epistemology, which most busy, impatient people aren't interested in listening to.

If I'm not making progress, I'm declining. You may think that if you're not growing, and continuously developing, then you're staying the same! Not so fast, hear me out. I've realised that if I'm not constantly doing the things to grow and develop myself, then that implies that I have neglected doing those things, which in a way also means that I'm receding. Why I say that is because our entire life is meant to be a journey of actualisation, development, and consciously increasing awareness. This process of *kaizen* is of constant and never-ending progress, and sometimes it may seem like you're taking 2 steps forward and 1 step backwards. That's what makes life and its odyssey an interesting yet challenging undertaking.

Just came across an Oscar Wilde quote on forgiving enemies, so this piece is a deconstruction of that, but from a whimsical perspective of spirituality.

You're fully spiritual when you're able to annoy the absolute hell out of others. It is sarcasm and mocking at its very best, and you cannot even tell that it's sarcasm or mocking. When the weak take offence and get upset, the spiritual forgives. When the weak make fun of, laugh and tease, the spiritual laughs with them. When the weak resist and fight, the spiritual passively acquiesces. The weak want to only win and not lose, the spiritual is beyond all such dualities. When they're crucifying the spiritual, the spiritual doesn't forgive them – because that'll be the ego forgiving – instead the spiritual asks the almighty to forgive them for being unaware. Again, the spiritual could say it in their own mind, but you have to annoy them, you see.

There's really nothing called discrimination or racism, only intelligence. You are either aware and intelligent, or not. Intelligence, not as in having intellectual knowledge, but rather from a point of view of awakened awareness – as in universal intelligence. Therefore, you're either awake, aware and intelligent or you're not.

If you are, then as much as you shouldn't forget the atrocities of the past, you must play your part in ensuring such atrocities are not meted out to the present and future generations. We've all come so far that at least much of the present generation does not use words that are discriminatory or racial, but would still behave or think discriminatively – at a subconscious level. So it's only a matter of time (I'm hoping not much) before we first start thinking impartially and evenhandedly, and then eventually becoming fair and equal to all – at a *being* level.

Remember that your prejudices against someone's nationality, caste, class, colour of skin, creed or financial worth, are all the outcome of your environment, conditioning and programming. Plus your own lack of intent, interest and desire to connect with the infinite intelligence that I've been referring to. Access to this universal intelligence is available to everyone, you only have to choose to merge and become one with it.

Stop. Take a break – from everything. Stop all activity. Don't do anything.

Well, you're always doing something. Even when you're not doing anything, you're still "doing" the "not doing", at least as a verb – whether it's sitting, or standing, or lying down or at the very least breathing. Okay, I've digressed enough.

Let's start again. Pause. Stop doing anything. No movement of any part of your body. Again, make sure absolutely no part of your body is doing any moving, other than your stomach expanding and contracting by the breathing. Ensure that your spine's erect and there's not even the slightest of movement of your fingers or toes or eyes or tongue. Even close your eyes if you want to, to avoid any blinking and to mentally focus on absolute motionlessness. Just stay that way, for as long as you want to. That's how you take a proper break.

Now, with that absolute stillness, put your attention on your thoughts, and wait for the next thought to arrive. At this point, if there's any saliva buildup in your mouth, either hold it, or very slowly swallow it, so that there's very little movement in your throat. Slowly. You are still absolutely still. Now put your attention back on to your thoughts, and wait for the next thought to arrive. Keep waiting, it'll come. Then wait again for the next thought. Keep waiting.

Spirituality and philosophy are closely related. I could even say one's synonymous with the other, or that one includes the other. Intellectually though, philosophy is regarded as the foundation of all knowledge, and combines both the arts (qualitative and subjective), and the sciences (quantitative and objective). Various subjects including languages and mathematics have emerged mainly for the discipline of philosophy to expand. Even the highest university degree, Doctor of Philosophy (Ph.D) is not limited to any specific discipline or subject.

Philosophy can be traced back to theories of ontology and epistemology, both of which are closely related to introspection and self-enquiry, which in turn are akin to spiritual investigation.

You're the one gathering and accumulating concepts and stories based upon your perspectives and understanding of reality. And your understanding of reality changes according to your open-mindedness, curiosity and inclusiveness.

I will also say that there's no outside doer of anything, you are the one experiencing yourself, giving yourself experiences and responding to those experiences. Which means there are only experiences. There's only *you* experiencing.

Remembering or forgetting is not within your control, it is not a choice you have. You can mentally let go of or not hold on to something, which is definitely under your control, but to completely erase it from your memory is not under your control. The passage of time or something extraordinary may sometimes lead you to forget situations or people, or you can choose not to allow someone or something to affect you mentally, but to forget something by *choice* is not possible. Likewise, we can choose to memorise, but to remember something is not under your control. You can put in all the effort to learn the multiplication table of 17 by heart, but to recall it is not within your control.

P.S. Falling asleep or waking up is not within your control.

P.P.S. What about birth and death?

Treat others the way they want to be treated, not the way you want to be treated. We're all different people, in terms of when and where we were born, how we were raised, the impact our parents, teachers, friends have had on us, and the various experiences we've had – there are too many variables. Which is probably why treating others the way you want to be treated may not be working for you.

Billions and billions of childbirths have taken place over the last thousands of years and the "ownership" of children has evolved from belonging to tribes and communities, to extended families to nuclear families. And as we progress and further evolve, the ownership would become more and more individualistic. Our children are not our property, we don't own them. They are individuals in their own right – they have their own compass. There's nothing wrong with them following it, and even making some mistakes in the process. Too much interference from people around them, especially parents, is causing a lot of distress among younger people. I say this from experience, I remember putting pressure on my daughter on two particular subjects, which she ended up losing interest in. Some parents even look to fulfil their own ambitions through their children, and compel them to follow the path they have set, which some children acquiesce to.

In a large way, we are products of our environment. What we as parents can do is provide our children with a supportive and encouraging ambience at home that is conducive and healthy for them to grow in. That's it. Remember that the fruit doesn't fall too far from the tree, and your children are more likely to become like you than like anyone else. Those little eyes are always watching you, so it's very important that you set yourself some good and high standards as an individual, and be that good fertiliser for your children to flower well.

P.S. Your children have chosen you for parents, and you have a responsibility towards them – you owe it to them.

This is how I feel now. These are my current perspectives and understanding. I feel I need to reiterate that everything I'm saying here is the result of all my introspection and enquiry – and these are interpretations of how I currently understand them. This may, or even may not change in the future, and I'm staying open to that.

Just got back from a run. Loved the nature – the trees, sounds of birds and the rain. Even spent some time observing an earthworm and a snail.

Brushing your teeth is one of the best mindfulness exercises – especially if you alternate between your left and right hands. Whether you brush once or twice a day, you habitually follow a certain pattern – you brush the front part, behind, and the chewing part, and there's rotation, up and down and sideways movement. What I'm suggesting is for you to follow the same patterns, however using the other hand as well. It can help integrate the two hemispheres of the brain, in order to accelerate learning and enhance performance in other areas.

In the middle of this winter, I decided to remove my socks just before getting into bed. After a few days of doing that, the signs and symptoms of my athlete's foot, however mild, started to alleviate. I no longer needed to use any topical lotion or cream after having a shower. I then stopped wearing socks even during the day, unless I was wearing shoes. Just the fact that my feet were getting some air and natural light had a big impact on my feet.

A few days thereafter, I came across a documentary on "grounding" or "earthing". I'd never heard of this concept, but it's a simple therapeutic approach that involves doing activities that "ground" or electrically connect you to the earth. Still quite under-researched at the moment, it's believed that through earthing or grounding – whether that's done by walking barefoot, lying on the ground, or even submerging in open waters – the natural defences of the body can be restored. So, walking and staying barefoot is my latest experiment. As I said, this study is in its infancy, yet some health professionals believe that the benefits of grounding may come simply by feeling like you're reconnected to nature. Regardless, there's little harm in giving it a go!

At some point I will
Write a beautiful haiku
That'll be the day

Take a lot of advice from motivational speakers and personal development teachers when you can. For as you make progress on this path, you cannot help but go deeper and broader into exploring the truth, self and consciousness, and the impediments and problems you'll face, can make you frustrated, confused and even depressed. You will hit one roadblock after another and feel disappointed that some of the pleasantness you once experienced is all gone. But trust me, keep licking your wounds and just keep at it – you will transcend them too.

You don't necessarily have to hit a low to rise. I hear stories of people having a turning point and then starting a new life – they say things like "I was at the lowest point in my life, couldn't go any lower and the only way was up". They generally relate it to a divorce or break-up, financial bankruptcy, major illness, losing a loved one, job loss etc. While these may be extreme circumstances, obviously the only way to transcend or get over them is by radically altering your own state of mind and your mental attitude, or by going within and waking up spiritually. However, sharing their personal "hero's journey" doesn't necessarily always help the listeners or viewers. Some people who feel they are at a low point may feel hopeful and inspired, however not everyone can relate to it. Not everyone has experienced their own lowest point. When an audience listens to such narratives there may be some who feel disappointed for not getting that turning point, or worse still wait for a low to hit them. The a-ha moment or epiphany can happen to anyone anytime regardless of their current situation – be it lowest, highest or somewhere in the middle.

In some cases, the realisation can happen after a series of experiences that may have occurred over years or decades. And it's not about getting the a-ha moment or epiphany, but what you do with it when it happens; more importantly for how long you keep doing it. Almost everyone encounters such moments frequently. But do they have the necessary prowess and agility to act on it, and keep acting on it for days, weeks, months and years until it brings out a new version of themselves? Personally, I'm not aware of hitting any low point, metaphorical or otherwise, but I got on to my own "hero's journey".

There is the conscious mind, and the subconscious mind; but what's this third something that is maintaining the physiology i.e. keeping the blood circulating, the heart beating and all the systems running? How's all this happening or who's behind all of this?

We know that the conscious mind is something we control with awareness and thought. The subconscious guides us based on our beliefs, past memories (including evolutionary and genetic) and past experiences – like driving a car. But again, who or what makes sure that our anatomy and physiology is functioning properly?

How can I get the most juice out of life? How do I live a truly full-fledged life? These were the kind of questions I used to ask myself (still do) as I researched life and its various components. I understand that I've only got one shot at life, and just like with each and every living being, my life will also come to an end. So, does that mean I should merely survive and exist until my dying day? Not at all! All the more reason to actually live it!

What we call a complete and full life is nothing more than a series of well lived days and profound experiences. So at least from a doing perspective, let's do everything we do with passion, enthusiasm and devotion, regardless of what it is that we're doing. Is that simple? Yes, not easy though – but you only get out of life what you invest and put in.

We need to spend more time learning about this only piece of life that we are. On the one hand it's important to learn, but it's also important to unlearn some aspects, i.e. to learn and introspect about the self, what truth is, what reality is, and to gently unlearn, or not hold on too tightly to any of our beliefs and education we've acquired through school, college and university.

One of the early experiments I conducted on self-healing was when I got knee pain and put an elastic brace strap on the good knee instead of the knee that was hurting; and in a matter of minutes, the hurting knee righted itself.

Self-healing is something I started learning and practising barely a few weeks into this journey of enquiry. I was understanding that pain is something that only I can feel, not the body. Now I can appreciate the connection between consciousness and health, and that wellness is a mere word, as well as illness. The fact that there's even the word "metaphysical" substantiates the connection between the subjective and the objective. Our psychology and more importantly our philosophy has some effect, if not a lot, on our physiology.

Note that the underlying state needs to be of inclusiveness and of surrender to all conditions; be that of illness or wellness. It's a way of living and being from that paradigm.

What I have found in my own life is that the harder I work on developing and improving my *inner* self – the metaphysical self like my mental attitude, personal philosophy, the choices I make and actions I take each moment – every aspect of my *outer* life corresponds to it. When I say "outer" life I mean areas like relationships, career, health, finance etc. We cannot have an outer life that is any bigger or better than our inner life. Life indeed is like a mirror and that to me is fantastic because it elucidates exactly the areas of my life that are growing and developing, and those that aren't.

.

Not all older people necessarily suffer from dementia or amnesia. Due to their age, or the stage they're at in their lives, they probably no longer feel the need to remember certain things at that point. On a subconscious level they may even *choose* not to remember names or labels, or they probably stop making an effort to recall them.

The Covid-19 pandemic has fully exposed how selfish we are as a people – from individual and community selfishness to national selfishness. I'm obviously not referring to universal or spiritual *Self*ishness – akin to universal love, which altogether transcends the duality of selfishness and selflessness – but the base selfishness that arises out of fear and lack. The mere fact that shelves at grocery stores and supermarkets get wiped out every time a lockdown is announced, regardless of how "developed" the country may be, fully validates this selfishness.

The real reason why we live in such a dystopian world is because of ego and selfishness. It's all about "me", *my* family, *my* community, *my* race, *my* suburb, *my* state, *my* country, without any holistic thinking or consideration for the whole.

It's all just a dream. Today I came across something that defined life as infinite imagination, and claimed that you didn't come from your parents, but that your parents came from your birth. You don't have to take my word for it, but let's contemplate and introspect on it.

The concepts of conception, birth and even death are something you learnt only after your birth. Had you not taken birth would this concept of birth and death even exist? You don't know. And how do you know for sure that your parents even existed before you were born? Concepts of evolution, science and history are all only concepts. The problem is that we don't question enough – especially the *most obvious* things. Having said all that, life is a dream, but it is also about waking up. And the best life is only possible when you're awake and able to live in the dream.

When I hear and read about conspiracy theories, I'm amazed by how myopic, biased and close-minded some people can be; to not only blindly believe such theories with total conviction, but to also promulgate them onto others. I'm not saying that all conspiracy theories are baseless, but most of them are.

I can say this now because there was a time, around 2004–05, when I got into all that in a big way and constantly kept digging for more and more conspiracies. I was in a mode of "false skepticism", not trusting anything or anyone, and was needlessly getting wrapped up in all the minutia.

To think outside-the-box is easier said than done, because even if you did, it would be within the confines of a bigger box. You see, we live our entire lives in a box filled with rules, morals, ethics, rights and wrongs, not to mention lists of things we are unwilling to be, do and have. All that, to only in the end be buried in that very box.

Remember, that we are on a "hedonic treadmill" and we tend to somehow always adapt. Everything elapses and passes away. Our attachment to things and people is much of the cause of distress, worry and anxiety. True outside-the-box thinking and living is when you're neither attached nor detached to anything, just like a droplet of water on a lotus leaf; it keeps dancing, but never sticks to the leaf.

Making the implicit explicit is what much of this journey is about – even if it means that you become philosophical doing it. Implicitly, we know that love, understanding, wisdom, joy, harmony, purpose, peace are all synonymous to living the good life, however unless we explicitly research and explore them, and actually live and embody them, we're only living in theory-land. Bear in mind that at some point it will be realised that not everything implicit can be made explicit, and that it's best to leave them implicit – consciousness for instance.

All I'm asking of you is to make an effort to go beyond absolutes and philosophies, and to just pay attention to your life and to all life, while sharpening your sense of perception. Observe, think less and be more connected. The more you think, the more disconnected you are with Being. In other words, the less you think, the more connected you are with Being. It's almost impossible to not think at all, given all our conditioning, but just try to imagine being in a state of no mind while you're still (and) alive. That's true liberation, that's *moksha*.

If you're being put on a pedestal, praised, and revered as a fully enlightened being, then you're not that. And if you enjoy or misuse that recognition, then you're no more than a mere celebrity looking for attention, fame and popularity. Whilst many such people may be enlightened, the fact that they expect "better cushions to sit on" speaks more of their pride and condescension, and less of their humility and simplicity. I'm not saying that humility necessarily trumps arrogance, but it just looks prettier from a spiritual standpoint.

Can you imagine meeting a fully enlightened person who after spending decades in contemplation, self-enquiry, meditation practices and spirituality, doesn't flaunt any of that? Yet their mere presence generates brilliance and light that radically alters your own way of being. They don't even talk about non-duality or consciousness or awakening – they live an "ordinary" life, yet in full awareness, knowledge and understanding of the Absolute.

P.S. I just finished reading *The 10 Ox-herding Pictures*, a book that describes the stages of a practising monk's progress towards full enlightenment, and their return to society.

Had I started to put together this book when I was in the initial stages of my "expedition", then almost everything I would've said would've been very positive and flowery. Since I am past that stage and have gone even deeper down the rabbit hole, I'm no longer as politically-correct or socially-skilled as I used to be. Although I do miss some aspects of those days, I'm now able to take it all in my stride, that things always move on and pass away.

Especially when you're on the path of enquiry and awakening, you understand that things always move in stages or phases. And I'm sure that this phase of mine will morph into something else, at some point. Until then, we all have to sit through this chapter of mine. You of course have the choice whether to sit through it or not – I don't.

There's only one thing you have as far as possessions go, and that's your body. The only object you truly own or possess is this thing called body. I'm not being figurative or philosophical, but literal – the only thing that really belongs to you is your body. So then what *are* you? You are life, consciousness, the intangible aspect that's inside and part of your body – that pervades throughout the body.

On a scientific level you are an inherent part of your body's every cell and atom. Since the intangible you cannot have experiences unless in a tangible body with sense organs, you i.e. consciousness gathered it. Your body cannot move a muscle or joint without *you* directing it. There has to be an element of you being involved in every movement. Note that you're not even the mind, thoughts or feelings – they're accumulations as well. So, if there's nothing *you* own or possess other than your body, the only thing you can nurture, care for and look after is your body, which is what we all do anyways. Absolutely everything we do revolves around ensuring that our body is in order – and we call that survival.

There was a time when I was exploring religion in a big way, and read many "holy" books of the popular world religions. And without being biased towards Hinduism (I don't really consider it to be a religion – it's more like a way of life like Yoga or Taoism), I must say that I found the content of the *Bhagavad Gita* quite unique and fascinating, mainly because it had almost nothing to do with religion and almost everything to do with consciousness and enlightenment. It's a wonderful guide for spiritual practice, showing the reader the path without influencing rituals and/or customs. But what stood out to me the most was, as if the scribe was none other than consciousness itself. I recall trying to read it back in maybe 2003–04 and found it quite hard to understand – I just didn't get it. However "post-shift", I was able to grasp a lot of it. More importantly, I understood that the Gita as a teaching is highly perspectival. Your own paradigms and perspectives play a very big role in how you understand and interpret it. Strangely, I kept finding "new" verses every time I was reading it; not that the book or its content was changing, but my understanding to absorb and perceive it was, according to 1) my state of mind 2) my perspectives and awareness, and 3) my ability to be open-minded and inclusive. I read it "religiously" for a few years, do so even now.

Here's a quote by Gandhi about the Gita: *"When doubts haunt me, when disappointments stare me in the face, and I see not one ray of hope on the horizon, I turn to Bhagavad Gita and find a verse to comfort me; and I immediately begin to smile in the midst of overwhelming sorrow."*

"Good, thanks. And you?!" The most common response when someone asks, "how are you doing?!"

Just this morning, while I was on my morning run, I overheard one say just that to another as they passed each other, and I went on to contemplate and reflect upon what it meant to say "I'm doing good".

Am I really saying in one word that each and every aspect of my Self is indeed good? Am I ignoring the subjectivity of the word good? Am I speaking of good health and well-being, and free of distress and pain? Am I being cheerful, amiable, optimistic, comfortable and peaceful? Am I saying that I am happy and grateful for what I have, am and do? Or am I in denial of all of the above, to simply respond with a "good, thanks. And you?!"

Enthusiasm is a tremendous state of being. Ponder on that word, keeping in mind that being happy is only an aspect of it.

Racism isn't just about putting down another race, even speaking up about a race is racism. Think about it, if you're speaking up about one race you're in a way speaking down on other races, because either way it is being said from a position of prejudice and judgment.

Most people, as asleep and close-minded as they are, will vehemently disagree with my viewpoint and stick to their presuppositions. Look, you can only excrete what you eat. Only what you put into your mind and body will come out of you, and if you're close- and narrow-minded or an absolutist, then that would mean that you're very selective about what you take in. You therefore become someone with limited knowledge and awareness. On the other hand, if you opened yourself a bit more, you're likely to have more perspectives, which could help you view things from a macro and holistic point of view. Unfortunately, much of humanity is too lazy and indolent to do so – it's far easier to live in a bubble or comfort zone than to do any work to increase general awareness and knowledge.

We are water. Our life began in water in our mother's womb, we then got on land, crawled on all fours, then walked on two; which is quite like the theory of evolution, which also began in water. But I think it should actually be called theory of chemistry, don't you think? Had a unit of oxygen, two units of hydrogen and the chemicals of earth not all merged, there wouldn't be any life. Therefore, our ancestors are not the great apes, but the blue-green algae – in fact water is really our ancestor.

How do we differentiate one life form from another and give them different labels? Isn't it by how they appear in shape and size, and how they move or travel? What has caused each of us to look different? Isn't it because of our desire to keep stretching? Not only in our existing environment but also in other conditions. Evolutionarily speaking, let's ponder on this important aspect of stretching to survive – starting right from the blue-green algae. Had these organisms not had the instinct to survive in their existing environment and the intrinsic intelligence to push themselves little by little on to other environments, then the millions of life forms would not have formed. Even we wouldn't be (t)here! So that begs the question if mind is the biggest factor in evolution. Or the only factor?

One of my favourite mindfulness, almost meditative, exercises is running. When I run, I focus on quite a few things – my breath, my stride, how close my heels are to my butt, if I'm pronating or supinating – if I'm leaning inward or outward as my feet hit the ground. I also try to catch the briefest moment of the glide.

The following is an important aspect, it's about paying close attention to the breath rhythm i.e. number of foot strikes for every inhalation, and exhalation – generally it's 3:4 (3 steps for one inhalation to 4 steps for one exhalation). Sometimes it drops to 2:3, or even 1:2 when I'm running faster. Some days I even do 4:3, 3:2 or 2:1, but how ever I do it, I prefer the odd number count, because it allows me to alternate my exhalation and inhalation between my left and right foot. Most of the breathing is done through the nose and mouth simultaneously, unless my mouth starts to dry up, when I inhale through the nose and exhale through the mouth.

Another thing I do is check my body posture – I prefer to lean slightly forward than running too straight. Also, when I'm running uphill, the natural tendency is to run on my toes. So as I'm doing all this, I'm basically not letting my mind wander too much, which is what I meant by mindfulness. I carry this mindfulness into how I finish the run, then into my post-run stretch, then into the shower, then into having my breakfast, and on and on into almost every activity for the rest of the day, whether I'm riding, driving, at work, at home, running errands or doing other chores.

Practising gratitude. Cultivating thankfulness and gratitude is a scientifically-backed way to increase happiness, and it's firmly within our control to be in a space of gratitude – verbal statements, affirmations or writing down a gratitude list are different ways of practising gratitude.

"Please don't judge me". I hear this line a lot especially from younger folk. I say (plead) to them: why the hell are you worried about being judged, and that too by people?! Let them have any notions about you. Live your life on your terms! The only thing you need to make sure of is that you're always on the side of Truth, and that the "integrity gap" is small, between:
- what you say and what you do,
- what you do and what you *should* do,
- what you're capable of being and doing, and what you're actually being and doing,
- your social self and your true self,
- how you think or feel you are, and how you truly are.

And the smaller the integrity gap, the better your life. It's a simple concept yet a profound one. So tell them: "go ahead and judge the hell out of me, but understand that in no way does it define me. It only defines you as judgemental".

Why do we look up to and revere heroes? Why is that we so want to become one ourselves? It's because the hero shows us our highest potential. Yet somehow, we just end up living out our mundane existence, by getting caught up in survival and pleasure activities and going for what's easy. The result? We end up blindly following the rest of the blind, and remain unfulfilled. Let me reiterate that no amount of external pleasures can satisfy the ego, it'll always keep wanting more.

Liberation and fulfilment are achieved only when the hero battles and overcomes the real villain, the one that resides within – that's how the "holy grail" is attained. A true hero is one who always sides with Truth – over ego.

Each of us gets the inspiration every now and then to stand up, stand out, become a true hero, and then inspire others to awaken. Each of us has the deep desire to fully connect to that muse inside of us, to become more aware, more conscious and encourage others as well. But then why don't we pursue it all the time? Because, almost all of humanity collectively serves the ego, and each of us are co-conspirators of the villain. Not to mention that it's not an easy process, it is hard! And we only want easy. We're constantly chasing easy, but keep getting the opposite.

P.S. The real heroes are not the sports stars, celebrities, movie stars, or politicians – they are the yogis, mystics and sages.

I am not entirely differentiating myself from others. We're all products of social conditioning, but many of us are in denial about it. Also, we aren't open enough to listening to our own intuitions, let alone someone else's.

Intuition is such a beautiful thing. Can you believe that out of nowhere, something that's somewhere within you gives you messages, suggestions and insights? And you as the perceiver or receiver is able to somehow capture this powerful infinite knowledge? Interestingly, it often doesn't use any language.

Any feedback is good, not just positive, because it goes to show that communication is taking place. But keeping quiet about someone's performance, or constantly putting off the discussion about how they're doing in their role, is nothing but poor management. If the feedback is positive, then all management has to do is encourage the employee to keep doing that, and if negative, provide help and suggestions to avoid doing them. Have that chat!

Employees who feel valued and appreciated by their managers are more likely to go above and beyond for the organisation, than those who don't receive any feedback from their superiors. They'll be happier in their roles, and are more likely to contribute towards the company's growth. If supervisors and team leaders are disregarding the importance of communication and connection with their employees, they're missing out on building a dedicated team that is likely to be with them for the long run.

Just because someone's on the spiritual path, they think they can say and do anything. They're on an enquiry trip, you see, and dare you say anything about them, because if you did they'll either be condescending or sarcastic to you. They may even be blasé about it and say something like "I know I'm wrong, and you're right". A "damned if you do, damned if you don't" kind of situation, right?

It should be pretty obvious that I'm also referring to myself here. I get it – it must be quite annoying and frustrating for people to deal with me, especially for those who know me well and have to interact with me a lot, like family members, friends and colleagues. But on the other hand, I feel that I upset people, mostly unknowingly. And that's one of the main reasons why I have chosen to stay tight-lipped about a lot of things or simply kept away from social gatherings, barring the occasional 1-on-1.

A lot of people give too much importance to work, and not enough to life. Hence the work/life imbalance. You don't have to get up to go to work; you get up because you found yourself to be alive, and you fully bask in that realisation. Going to work just happens to be another thing in the day.

Work is no more or less important or unimportant than anything else. Remember there's only life, in which work is only a component.

Every part of Earth, every piece on Earth has been created equally – no place is less or more holy or unholy than any other. We're all citizens of Earth. No country belongs to anyone, yet every country belongs to everyone. People may have drawn lines and created political boundaries, but we can choose, at least in our own minds, to not have any kind of separation or boundaries. And of course, identity is the other issue. Let me tell you, if you're one of those that doesn't believe in god or religion, but does so in whatever country you identify with, you are still ideological and dogmatic, as well as oblivious and clueless about your conditioning on such concepts and constructs, like a label of a country.

I was a part-time driver partner in a rideshare company for about 4½ years; I did it mainly as an avocation, and must say it was one of the best things I've ever done. I did about 4500 trips and got to go to new places, meet new people, and have fresh conversations with them. I've chatted with sports stars, CEO's, musicians, gangsters, chefs, bakers, stand-up comedians, escorts, prostitutes, tourists, filmmakers, actors, monks, lawyers, policemen, airline pilots, flight attendants, tattoo artists, copywriters and many other interesting people. I can't think of any other part-time job that provides as much flexibility and freedom as does rideshare-driving – you can pick your own hours, and turn the app on or off at your own choosing. I really encourage you to sign up, if there's ridesharing available in your city. More than anything else, do it as a side-hustle just for personal development, while making a bit of money. It'll provide a newness to your week; you'll learn to become more flexible and accommodating, and most importantly you can develop your ability to go with the flow, rather than to always be in control.

I must admit that ever since I've been on this quest, barring several awakening and mystical experiences, there's been only one instance when I was able to actually make sentient union with consciousness. It happened so randomly one day, and I completely merged with infinite consciousness, which lasted for a good few seconds, well at least it seemed like only a few seconds. I was in a space of emptiness, there was only the now, an everlasting present moment, without any concepts, thoughts or language.

If not for my 5 senses, most importantly the sense of touch, I wouldn't even know if I exist. I know I'm a living entity only because I can see, hear, smell, taste and feel – the first 4 of the sense organs happen to be on the face; the sense of touch however, is experienced by the whole body, not just by our hands and feet. Can you even remotely imagine a life without any senses? We wouldn't have a clue about anything at all!

First saying: "I know that's such a first world problem", then following it up with a chuckle. It just sounds wrong. And even if you're one of those "grateful" types and are "compassionate" towards the underprivileged, you still don't get it. The only people who really get it are the underprivileged, who are living in that very situation. Unfortunately, such disparity will continue to be blatant as long as government policies are economically-driven, and are mostly tipped in favour of the rich.

We live in such an unfair, unjust and partial world where there are individuals who are richer than even some nations. This gross inequality that exists in our world is absolutely crazy and makes me sick in the stomach. Every now and then (like right now), I get highly overwhelmed by sheer guilt for living in such comfort, when I know that there are people and children who don't even know what a house is; that I sometimes waste food and water when I know that there are animals, children and others who are malnourished and dying because of lack of water or food. Don't assume that just saying "I know it's a first world problem" takes away any of your arrogance! It only speaks about your conceit and pride, and not about your humility or gratitude.

It's obviously very obvious that most of the privileged live a privileged life only because they were lucky to be born and raised in a privileged community or country, which most of them completely disregard, and take for granted. Read that line again. They could've been born in an underdeveloped country and be raised in abject poverty, but they just don't seem to get it. The way most of them walk, talk and behave is as if they're entitled to the privileges. You might be saying: "okay, I get it, but what do you want me to do?" Nothing, really. I'm only ranting, but it is exasperating to constantly see division everywhere, mainly economic. Well, if nothing else, just be more appreciative and humble – not when it's convenient for you, but all the time, for the rest of your life!

I wouldn't disagree if you think that I'm hiding behind this book. If you think I'm having double standards – by saying everything I want to say to people through this book, but not to their faces, you're probably right. If you're going to judge me as a hypocrite for constantly criticising others yet not myself, I may not protest that either, although I do believe that I'm quite critical of myself.

That being said, I definitely did talk about all this to others, but I would always upset and put them off, and even myself. However, now when I say the same things via a medium such as this book, then a) I don't directly offend them, b) I'm able to take the time to explain and express myself better, and c) the reader is able to process them better. Let me reiterate that I'm always trying to be on the side of Truth – which many of you may think to be perspectival, which in truth isn't – and therefore I don't believe I'm doing anything wrong by saying what I'm saying. I'm not offering a panacea i.e. to resolve or find solutions to all problems, but only trying to find ways to handle and face them. And by the way, the only people who don't have any problems are dead.

You are not *what* you eat and drink, but *how*. You can tell a lot about someone by how they drink and eat. I'm not only referring to eating and drinking etiquette or table manners, but I'm coming from a position of mindfulness and awareness. And it doesn't really matter what you're eating or drinking – everything is inherently neutral. Although, as you master this art of consuming, you will automatically start paying attention to the *what* as well. Intaking is one of, if not *the* most important activity of your life, and it's important how much attention, presence, awareness and reverence you give to it.

Anyways, isn't it time that in general we started moving away from many such whats, and towards the hows? It's not what you do, but how. It's not what you say, but how. It's not what you see, but how. It's not what you are, but how.

Here's a list of my favourite books:

The Monk Who Sold His Ferrari – Robin Sharma

The Power of Now – Eckhart Tolle

Man's Search for Meaning – Viktor Frankl

Power vs Force – Dr David Hawkins

The Eye of the I – Dr David Hawkins

As a Man Thinketh – James Allen

Bhagavad Gita

Sapiens – Yuval Noah Harari

Ten Ox-Herding Images – Wim Van Den Dungen

Personal space doesn't just mean physical space. It includes space of all kinds. Even if I speak too loudly, I'm encroaching on your personal space. This is something I notice a lot when I'm out jogging or taking a walk, and people around me are talking loudly with no consideration for others' personal space. It even happens at grocery stores and shopping malls, not to mention at sporting events and movie theatres.

To take it even further and possibly sound crazy, if I'm in your visual space or even in your mind, that is also an intrusion into your personal space.

I started journaling (diary-writing, as I used to call it) in my tweens, and diligently kept it going for about 10 years. In the initial years, I was just jotting down things I did each day, like a record of my daily activities. There wasn't really anything private or personal in it, which of course changed as I was getting into my mid to late teens. And after that I'm not sure what happened, but my writing became infrequent. I guess life happened and my priorities changed, and slowly but surely my journaling completely stopped. It was only in 2012 that I got back into it, this time in a very big way. In fact, much of what you're reading here is straight out of my journal. I've written hundreds of pages on a variety of topics and continue to do so.

If you haven't journaled, I would highly recommend it. It is a great form of self-expression – to pour out, not all but your most important insights, thoughts, ideas and feelings onto a page. It can result in many positive outcomes and improvements to the quality of your life, because what you're doing is authentically and sincerely enhancing the relationship with yourself and your mind. *Writing doth maketh an exact man.*

Every time you suppress or repress your thoughts and emotions, please don't think you've gotten rid of them. You're very much still holding them in your body. And don't immediately conclude that you're holding them in your brain or heart. You're actually holding them in your entire anatomy and physiology – on a subatomic level. All those thoughts and feelings, whether subtle or obvious, small or big, positive or negative, will express themselves homeostatically i.e. through physical or mental wellness or illness. They have to find expression in one way or another, for they're all within you, they're part of you – they are you! And all those metaphysical aspects of you can express themselves physically and visibly only through your very own physiology. You could use words to express them by speaking or writing them out. However, bear in mind that no language has the ability to express all your feelings and thoughts fully.

What I'm trying to articulate with great difficulty, is that we're always experiencing, and then responding to those experiences. If we are by nature only experiencing and taking in objectively with keen discernment, then that's like being in a state of mindfulness or even meditation. If we're not paying any attention to the experiencing and only reacting (often with a flight, fight or freeze response), then we're in a state of unconsciousness – living in the past and future, rather than in the present.

Being vegan or vegetarian is your choice, and it depends on how important any ideology is to you, to label yourself one or the other – even to label yourself as a carnivore, for that matter. Bear in mind that there are starving children who don't have that choice. Therefore, merely having that choice is a privilege you enjoy, and utilising it makes you sort of snooty, to put it mildly. My question is if you really need to label yourself as anything at all. Also note that if you're moralistic about one thing but not another, then your conscience is not entirely sincere.

Much of the problem here is due to a) a lack of holistic thinking and b) an attachment to the *label* of vegan, vegetarian, or carnivore. I'm neither condemning nor celebrating whatever you eat, but I feel that being an ideological crusader and trying to impose your values about food and diet onto others isn't really necessary. As much as food plays a very important part in our lives, is there really a need to campaign about it?

Does eating or not eating animal products make you an unconscious or a conscious person? I don't think it's that clear-cut. Awareness and consciousness is beyond any such dualities, prejudices, absolutisms, and all isms. There's a popular law school saying that goes: "always avoid always, and never say never".

As for me, I don't even know how I'd label myself. I'm all labels yet none. Figure that out!

Again, remember that the most important relationship is the one you have with yourself. Your career can only fulfil that part of you where you can express your creative thinking. Money can only do so much, because once you hit your number, you will just want more. The material things you own or wish to own can only bring you temporary satisfaction. Even relationships with family and friends are non-permanent. Therefore it comes down to the one and only relationship, the one with oneself. The more time we spend developing things outside of us like career, relationships, family, the less time we will have in nurturing our own Self. But the more time we spend in developing the relationship we have with our true Self, the more the things on the outside will get enhanced, and the more meaningful and fulfilling our life will become. Personal development, spirituality, wellbeing, self-enquiry, actualisation, awakening, enlightenment is not a side dish; it's the main meal, in fact the only meal.

Live your life in such a way that you don't need to say thanks, please or sorry. I'm not suggesting to *live* without being grateful, humble or remorseful. Not at all. In fact, the most conscious, spiritual and actualised life is only possible when you fully embody these qualities and are grounded in states of gratitude, humility and remorse. It's probably the simplest way to live the good life. I'm referring to the *saying* of these "magic" words, and how they're used in most contexts today – frivolously and without sincerity. Have you heard some parents say to their children: "Now what do you say?!" These parents think they can discipline their children by simply getting them to make those sounds without actually teaching them to live those words. How many of these parents even live them?

The reason a lot of my content radiates frustration and annoyance is because much of my current world triggers just that. To me this world appears to be quite asleep, foolish and unaware, not to mention inauthentic and fake. And the worst part is that nobody shows any intent to become otherwise. In these times of Covid-19 lockdowns with little social interaction, the people I mainly engage with are those at work, and I keep getting ridiculousness, almost all the time. What's become blatantly evident from this pandemic is how much of a poor relationship each of us has with our own self. They say, you are/you become your environment – your level of consciousness and awareness is largely dependent upon the majority of people you observe, listen to and interact with. Most of my time in solitude is spent reading, writing or contemplating about life and reality, and all that has resulted in me becoming "high maintenance". Yes, I have and live by certain values and principles, however the moment I step into the "real world" all that comes crashing down. Almost everyone tends to violate these values and standards, almost all the time. Therefore, if all I did was only absorb, tolerate and take in all the BS and not find a way to vent, express and release them, I would become an even bigger wreck. Putting everything down into this journal is definitely helping. I am fully aware that much of it has to do with my own perspectives and judgements. Yet on another level, people are just not willing to take responsibility to become truly flexible, open-minded and inclusive.

Most of today's education is based on memorisation, especially at the primary and secondary levels. Not just with languages and mathematics, but also with humanities, sciences and even creative subjects. And the child's success or progress depends a lot on their cramming abilities. But in today's technologically-advanced world – where search engines can help us with almost anything and everything – epistemology, raising awareness, developing knowledge, creativity and understanding have all become way more important than just developing memory.

My heart breaks when I see pet-owners, mainly of dogs, walk their pets. It is shocking; they just don't seem to care or bother about the life walking next to them. They're so busy talking, walking, being on their phone, or just unaware – it's crazy! Some even use fear-inducing or dominating tactics and threats to discipline their dogs.

I say to them, don't own a pet if you can't look after them like your child, or yourself. And then there are some who are at the other extreme, who are constantly pampering the pet, when it's convenient for them without any consideration for the animal. The way you treat your pet speaks a great deal about your own awareness and consciousness – mostly your lack of it.

Weapons have always played a large role in humanity and civilisation, and in the way they've shaped us as individuals and as a society. However, guns and firearms in particular have completely transformed the world in which we live today. They've been one of the most (adversely) significant inventions in the history of the world, especially when you take into account how explorers and colonisers have used them.

Sometimes it's pure serendipity.

We've all heard anecdotes about film stars, musicians, sportspersons finding their big break often because of someone else's misunderstanding or misfortune. Even the Wright Brothers and the airplane – apparently, there were many other experimenters who were working on flying airplanes at the time, but it was the Wrights that came up with the right ideas at the right time that made them the inventors of the world's first motor-operated airplane.

It's a similar kind of story with Roger Bannister and the 4-minute mile. I'm guessing it would've been something similar even with the story of the Buddha. I'm sure there would've been many others at the time who may have had awakening and enlightenment experiences, especially in a place like India that has always been known as a country of seekers. However, the fact that Gautama was the son of a king – who had sacrificed all worldly luxuries to understand reality – may have actually worked in his favour. With all due respect, note that in all the above scenarios I'm not taking away the hard work, effort, talent and perseverance that these people have put in. Sometimes, you're just at the right place at the right time when something right happens.

Every morning, check if your joints are working properly, and if you're able to move all of them. Be gentle while checking, without jerky movements.

Check if you're able to move all your toes. Check if you're able to move and rotate your ankles, clockwise and counterclockwise. Can you move and rotate both knees? What about your hips – can you swing your legs forward and backwards, and sideways? And your lumbar region, can you rotate it, can you bend forward, backwards and sideways? Next, your shoulders – can you lift your arms forward, sideways and rotate them? Can you rotate both elbows, and wrists? And can you move all joints in your hands? Next, your neck – check if you can, very gently and slowly, move it in all directions and rotate it? Lastly, your jaw – check if you can move the mandible vertically and horizontally?

Here's a rant on how some businesses operate – they just don't care about you. All they care about is your money, and themselves. Their main and perhaps only job is to take advantage of your helplessness. You go to them for something, and they hook you in and find sneaky ways to get your money. Once they're successful in doing that, there ends their commitment and responsibility towards you. They will almost never keep their word, or keep you in the loop of what's happening. You have to keep following up with them over and over again. And if at all they apologise, you'll probably get the most blasé and nonchalant "sorry".

Bear in mind that you're considered the one at fault when you point out to them that they're not keeping their promises or following on their commitment. They can keep falling back on their promises, but dare you *tell* them that!

I cannot cajole you or give you motivational advice, I'm sure there are enough teachers who can do that for you. I'm here to disturb and shake the deepest part of you, your very core, and I may even injure it with some of my words, but that's the only way I can get you to look within; that's the only way you can catch even the slightest glimpse of reality. Yes, it is possible for anyone to fully understand reality, but only if you're able to first clearly see and become aware of all the impeding distractions that the asleep society has for you, so as to keep you from waking up and actualising. Distractions like career, family, friends, media, smartphones, movies, advertising, video games, social media, junk food, sport, porn, conspiracy theories, alcohol… should I keep going?!

So, once you realise that it is possible for you to understand reality, and also become aware of all the red herrings, you'll be off to the races. From then on, you won't need any guru or teacher, for you will have found your most important teacher – your Self.

You're not always thinking. Many times thoughts occur *to* you, and you happen to be the listener, heeder or perceiver of that information. This may sound strange, but it happens to me a lot, especially when I'm taking a shower, reading a book or on a walk – some fascinating new insights occur to me, and I go "wow!" I'm sure it happens to you too, you may call them intuitions, but how ever you put it, they happen *to* you. And you wouldn't have been able to catch them unless you were consciously open to them.

Top-notch celebrities like movie stars, sports stars, politicians, TV presenters, writers, and even some journalists may have all the fame and fortune, and in some cases even a cult following, but all said and done they still identify themselves with their profession, industry or country. Pardon me for saying that even the military personnel serving their country's defence forces, and laying down their lives is all done out of "identity" and "separation" – the two main components of the ego, be it individual or collective. Some celebrities even become philanthropists and flaunt their generosity, which may all be commendable, but they still do it with an egoistic bias.

Nothing against the people above, but there is a minute fraction of people in almost every part of the world who've broken through all or any such identities, biases and prejudices – most of all their ego. These are the sages, monks, yogis and mystics, who are mostly unknown.

A few months into this odyssey, I came up with an acronym – HEAD which stood for Humility, Enthusiasm, Appreciation, Discipline.

H: When you're humble, you're in a space of acceptance and open-mindedness and you don't really mind how things pan out – you just do everything with the best intentions and take what you get, knowing well that regardless of the result you've grown and learnt a lot.

E: Enthusiasm is not to be confused with happiness. It is but an attitude with which you do things. What I'm referring to is more about being inspired and taking action with eagerness and excitement, and also with warmth.

A: Appreciation is not so much using the words "thank you", not even just thinking and feeling thankful, but truly *being* in a space of thankfulness, yet having a sense of acknowledgement and understanding of gratitude.

D: To be truly successful, you have to exert both internal and external types of discipline. Internal being self-restraining and differentiating right from wrong, and external being adhering to societal norms, including following the law. Whilst you behave in a consistently controlled manner, you also bring stability and structure into your life. Self-discipline is a form of freedom from laziness and lethargy.

Woe is me. We're all just victims. Have you noticed, every time you have an argument or altercation with someone close to you, both of you are trying to "out-victim" one another. "You did or said that, so that makes me the victim", "but that's because you did or said that, so am I not the bigger victim here?" And on and on it goes.

If traffic authorities really want to penalise offenders by financially hurting them, then the traffic fines have to be a certain percentage or proportion of the offender's net income or net worth, not just a flat amount. A fine of $200 would really hurt someone earning $500/week, but not at all to someone making twenty times more.

High integrity is what we expect from everywhere. We only want to deal and interact with those with high integrity.

What is integrity, after all? It is the quality of being honest and having strong moral principles. A more profound definition is that it's a state of being whole and undivided.

So whether we're at work or among family and friends, whether we're dealing with a business or even at a restaurant for a meal, we expect everyone to be integrous and highly reasonable. Primarily because we've concluded that *we* are that, and therefore don't expect anything less in return.

Note that when you point a finger at someone, you're pointing three at yourself.

What astounds me nowadays is when I see genuine kindness, authenticity and integrity, in a world that is abound in fabrication and falsehood.

Ever since I've been on this path, my understanding and perception of almost everything has undergone a radical shift, and it continues to evolve and change. I do view things from a different angle now. Arrogantly speaking, "from above", and with more clarity and awareness. Hence, I fully understand that I am the biggest "problem" in my life – not anything or anybody else. I notice things more than I ever did, including (especially) my own deficiencies and inadequacies. So it's only obvious that anything that's sincere, genuine and true will jump out at me.

I keep harping on about the fact that everyone is actually on the same path, so should I then, as a "seeker", not do my bit to open their eyes to that reality?

Should I not help them change their existing obtuse worldview?
Should I not stop them from blindly sticking to the herd?
Should I not encourage them to venture into unknown territory?
Should I not inspire them to experience true reality through direct experience?

In the past, especially during the first few years, I would verbalise and vocalise my thoughts and feelings, but now I just pour them out into my journal, which is what you're currently reading.

No matter what I say or how much I say, you're the one who has to get it. I mean you have to really really get it! And you can only get it, when you're totally open and inclusive. And honestly, it's not easy, which is why there are more deluded and asleep people than awake ones. First of all, something deep within your subconscious has to shake and shudder, like a simple a-ha moment *(kenshō)*, which is only a wakeup call, but then you have to keep at it and "stay awake" for at least a few months for things to start shifting within you *(satori)*, and then sustain it for a few more years and you'll start getting glimpses of reality and even have some mystical experiences.

I will warn you though that *kenshō* and *satori* aren't enough – you will need to deepen these experiences even further and bring it to maturation. How? By increasing your intellectual understanding through reading, journaling, introspection, meditation and contemplation. Then you will have enlightening experiences again and again, which you will need to continuously support with deliberate practice upon practice. With all that done, it's guaranteed that you will awaken – not with death, but while still living.

My understanding and practising of inclusiveness started when my daughter was in her final year of high school. As her year 12 exams were approaching, and she was spending much of her waking hours in preparation, my anxiety and concern for her started to grow. I was hoping she would do well in her exams and come out tops. Until one morning it dawned on me that the concern I had for her, and my desire for *only* her to do well was very selfish. That I was unperturbed about her friends, or other year 12 students in her school, or even all year 12 students in other schools. That I was not bothered about students who were preparing for exams and tests all around the world, or about people who were working on achieving their goals in every field.

My thinking and understanding of self-biases started becoming deeper and wider, as I realised that I had to become more considerate and thoughtful of everyone equally; to broaden the boundaries of what I consider me and mine – to become inclusive.

Another acronym I created many years ago was EIGHT – like the sign of infinity but vertical, and it stood for being infinitely:

Enthusiastic
Inspired
Grateful
Humble
Trusting

One may think that the spiritual way is something that organisations, companies and governments couldn't follow, and that it only applied to the few individuals who are actually on the path of "seeking". That's how myopic most people are; not realising that absolutely everything organisations do is on the lines of spirituality, and is done to become a spiritually intelligent organisation.

Let me also clarify that spirituality is not just about sitting in a yoga pose and meditating, that's only one aspect. It is, in fact, a way of consciously living, functioning and being in a space of holistic awareness, knowledge and oneness about every aspect of existence and life.

You may be noticing how more and more conscious companies are slowly but surely getting on this path of organisational enlightenment.

We know that it takes about 40 weeks for the human embryo to fully develop, come out of the womb and be seen by the world. Similarly, if you put in the 6700 hours of effort and practice into anything and consistently made progress, then there's a very good chance you will master it, and get noticed by the world.

Did you know that the yardstick used to measure how developed a country is, is based on infrastructure, economic stability and comfort, not awareness or consciousness? As an awakening adult, I don't see a lot of conscious, aware or even awake people anywhere, no matter how "developed" a country they live in. You may be living in a highly "developed" city or country, but unless you're developed or even developing within, your confidence and pride in the external environment doesn't matter at all.

I cannot stress enough that no amount of material possession or money can give you real happiness and contentment. Nor can fame. It's just not possible. The fact that there are more depression and mental health problems in "first world countries" corroborates that fact. Let me also reiterate that mental wellness or illness is not happening outside of the physical you, but within. If only people understood what I'm trying to say – most live their lives in a grey zone, chasing their tails, staring into screens, and waiting to take offence.

Ever since I have been on this path of actualisation, I've tried to utilise my morning hours to the fullest. I get up early, and spend the first few hours in solitude and in nature – not just pondering about and contemplating nature, but actually being in absolute awe of its wonder. Regardless of whether it's a weekday or the weekend, I go out first thing. It's beautiful to catch the breaking of dawn. I've always been lucky with flexible work hours, often not having to start early.

Almost all of humanity wakes up only to go to work, not to catch the first rays of the sun, listen to the birds, enjoy the solitude, enjoy the silence, and be alone with the source, without any distractions. I don't really do it only to feel good, but to catch a new sense of awareness. *A new sense of awareness.*

A Cinquain:

I
Selfish, Selfless
Having, Doing, Being
There is only one
Ego

One of the difficult aspects of this work, as counterintuitive as it may sound, is having compassion, sympathy and concern for others. Of course, during the early stages of personal development, you may find it quite easy to be understanding and compassionate of others – you may even go do some volunteer work of helping the poor, sick and needy. However, as you delve deeper into self-enquiry and spirituality, you somehow start to go in the opposite direction. This is mainly because you've started to understand the concept of inclusiveness and non-duality, and don't see yourself as being separate from others.

Any inadequacies, unawareness and unconsciousness you see around is actually all in you – not figuratively, but literally. And this makes you frustrated, and to a degree misanthropic. Although you may understand inclusiveness, you still have an egoic self which hasn't been fully softened or mastered. Until then, be prepared to be misunderstood, underestimated and even ridiculed.

Jealousy or envy is a strong feeling, and with "social media jealousy" happening everywhere, it can, to a very large extent be answered: with awareness. Yes, with awareness – fully recognising that this is happening to you, by completely embracing and understanding all the mental chatter and feelings it brings with it.

I'm not saying that feeling jealous is bad or good, it's just a feeling like happiness or sadness, and it's not happening without or outside of you, but only within. Read that line again. All these thoughts or feelings are yours and nobody else's, and all you can do is fully include and accept them, and not suppress or change them, which will allow them to pass. Read that line again and again.

Recently at a mall, I saw a child throw a tantrum, and the mother was scolding and reprimanding the child to stop doing it. An older lady watching this walked up to the mother and suggested something to her, and boy did she flip her lid – "how dare you tell me what to do?! I will raise my child the way I want to, you mind your own business!"

I reflected on the above incident, and how such scenes take place in a society that is low conscious. In a high-conscious society, each of us would have the right to police or intercept any kind of emotional or physical abuse, whether that's meted out towards a child, adult or even a pet. We're all part of the same community and making it conducive to live in is each one's duty. There's nothing like "this is my child, my partner or my pet, I'll do or say whatever I want, and you have no right to interfere in my affairs". That is nothing but selfishness, ego and unawareness.

When you're doing a 5k, 10k, half-marathon or full, you tend to hit the runner's wall about three quarters of the way in. For as you get closer to your destination, or any goal for that matter, you tend to become more anxious, tired and doubtful. That's when you need to be present on the journey, rather than focus on the destination.

Settling down. Why? What does that even mean? Constantly evolving and changing is the way, maintaining a sense of adventure and flexibility. *Kaizen* is the process of continuous and ongoing development and improvement.

Most people think they know enough to be a pessimist, but not enough to be an optimist. That's the kind of negativity that pervades within humanity. I think we just don't know enough to be either. And that's okay, it's a good place to be – of *not* knowing (as much as I keep stressing the importance of increasing awareness). But if you haven't bothered finding out or exploring, then your understanding and perspectives remain narrow and limited.

It's counterintuitive that the more you know, the more you know that you don't know enough. Somewhat like travelling – the more you travel the more you feel you haven't travelled enough.

Perspectives and viewpoints can change with time. Some change over decades, some over years, some even over months or weeks. I'm not talking about an aha or eureka moment that causes a change of mind or preference, but I'm referring to a *paradigm shift*. This is when your usual way of thinking about or doing something is replaced by a new and different way, and there's a major change at a conceptual level. Events such as 9/11, GFC or even Covid-19 are considered paradigm-shifting events.

The reason I'm alluding to this topic here in my journal is because such a shift can occur in individuals. This shift is very evident and obvious when you're on the path of actualisation, spirituality and self-enquiry. But even when you aren't actively or consciously pursuing that path, it still can happen to you. The most modest or unassuming of events or comments can trigger it, however, the paradigm shift only happens if the recipient takes it on, embraces it, sustains and carries it forward for a very long period of time.

P.S. There are entries in this journal that do not sit well with me at the moment, but vehemently did when they first occurred to me.

The conundrum is that before I got on this path of waking up, I perceived everything like the people around me, however once I got on the path, my perceptions and understanding of reality started to change. I discovered that I had taken a detour – but when I looked around there was no one else with me. I was by myself. This, I was able to ascertain only in hindsight, not when I had actually taken that detour. Before the "shift", I was the result of everything that was fed to me by family, school, university, media, colleagues, friends etc. However, post-shift, I took it upon myself to make epistemology the most important subject to study, and to truly understand reality from the perspective of truth and consciousness – all beyond beliefs and conditioning, and beyond the finite confines of any language.

Who am I to forgive you? You have done no wrong, so there's no need for me to forgive you. Who am I to get offended? You have done no wrong, and there's no need for me to get offended. I can only take offence to myself, which also means there's only self-forgiveness.

If you've never meditated before and wish to start a meditation practice, then what I can suggest is to use the calendar as a guiding tool. On the 1st of the month, meditate for one minute, then for two minutes on the 2nd, for three on the 3rd and so on. The key is to not overdo or underdo it, unless you have successfully done it for a few months; that's when you can double the duration i.e. 2 minutes on the 1st, 4 on the 2nd and so on. See how you go.

A rhetorical question: how does nature perfectly balance itself? If there are cold places on Earth, there are almost equivalent warm places. If there are dry places, there are almost equivalent wet places. It has nothing to do with political boundaries or countries.

Consciousness or god or universal intelligence is in no way biased towards one or another region. It's holonic, and it's doing what it needs to do to bring a general balance and homeostasis everywhere. Even natural "disasters" like hurricanes, tornadoes, volcanic eruptions, earthquakes, tsunamis, and storms are actually consequences of everything the Earth is naturally doing to stabilise imbalances. We call them "natural disasters", but they're basically natural occurrences, and they've been happening for millennia. But now that the human population is up by crazy numbers, we're everywhere, and are bound to come in nature's way, which sadly results in loss of life, and other calamities including economic calamity.

Becoming spiritual has nothing to do with your behaviour or your words, but about how you *are* as an individual. I may talk all spiritual, but from a societal perspective, I am probably less polite or nice than I used to be. I've lost some of my social skills like polite language and nice behaviours, as well as calling and checking up on family and friends, but I'm more at peace and ease with myself than I've ever been. Only because I am on the side of Truth and authenticity. And I don't expect everyone to understand this. Whether they get it or not, I'm okay either way.

Let me say this (most of you may disagree): each and everyone is a spiritual being. However, you consciously take the spiritual path only when there occurs a transformation within you. You become more and more open-minded and inclusive, and your sense of identity goes beyond the confines or dimensions of what you had until then considered yourself to be – the physical you.

Understand this: any identity is finite, whereas you are infinite.

Some people I interact with are so bitter and sour that I cannot even put into words. Some of them are like a volcano waiting to erupt. Unfortunately, such people will continue to be bitter and evoke, promote and rear similar people and perspectives around them, whether that's in their homes, workplace or socially. Sad, but true. It could take generations of suffering, sickness and misery before we can see any light coming through all this. Unless there is a sudden surge of awakening and consciousness.

Dog lovers say OMG, cat lovers OMT :-)

Imagine taking away concepts of the clock and the calendar i.e. no seconds, minutes or hours and no months, weeks or dates. All there is, is days becoming nights, nights becoming days, changing of the seasons, and the lunar cycles. It's fascinating to view and perceive nature and life devoid of the watch and calendar, and of all numbers.

Thanks, sorry, please, male, female, father, mother, son, daughter, brother, sister, wife, husband, friend, colleague, stranger, Monday, Friday, past, present, future, earth, India, Australia, Portugal, cancer, diabetes, asthma, leg, hand, brain, heart, birth, death are all only words. They're all just words and labels from the English language, and do not mean anything more than what they really are – mere words. I am being literal here.

When I take offence – which is quite often – to some of the things people say or how they behave, they immediately defend themselves by saying how much respect and reverence they have for me, and that I'm the one misunderstanding them. I know that the kind of respect they're talking about is a very conditional one, and just because they "say" they respect me, they feel entitled to do or say anything they want. Such people don't really respect anyone unconditionally, they only like to talk about their respect. I say, why bother with all this? Just don't look up to anyone or look down upon anyone, no matter who that is.

You are as much a tyrant, dictator, terrorist or villain as you're a sage, prophet, monk or a mystic. Let me ask you: who has seen, heard, learnt or read about these people? You. Where do all these people exist? Only in your mind. Who's the one judging them as good or bad people? You are. Is it all sounding like solipsism? Probably, but only *you* think that those others are separate from you. Think about this: if you were not there, if you didn't exist, if you didn't have senses or a mind, then the tyrant or sage wouldn't exist either. There's *only* you – the one that identifies yourself, who is separate from others.

No one likes to be caught doing the wrong thing. At carnatic music concerts and other gigs, I see people, generally musicians themselves or critics, sit right in the front row and chit-chat away, laugh and actually have random discussions while the concert's going on – without giving any regard for the people around them or the musicians performing on stage. It is disappointing, actually disgusting. And the worst part is that they will take offence if you told them to stop it – to shut up or get out. Instead of feeling ashamed and apologising they will give you a look of "how dare you!" You know why they get offended? Because they've been caught, and shown how unconscious and unaware they really are. Or they might even laugh it off, to fully show their lowest self.

Just like every nation is a developing nation, each and every person is an awakening person. There's no such thing as an underdeveloped country or a developed country – every country is always in the process of constantly developing. Similarly, each of us is in the process of awakening. There never was, is or will be a fully awakened person or a fully developed country; we as individuals and a collective are always in the process of evolving, realising and growing all the time.

Gender-neutrality should be fully experimented in the field of sport, where and when possible. Ability, competency and skill should be the only determining factors of who gets picked for the team or side, regardless of their gender. A "world number one" in any sport is not really a world number one until they have been tested by all opposition. We cannot, but more importantly should not, make any assumptions about the result, if opposing genders are asked to compete – we just don't know. For starters, this could be experimented in gymnastics, archery, fencing, snooker, billiards, car and motorcycle racing and equestrian events. Subsequently, it can be trialled in other sports like soccer, cricket and tennis. In a few decades, gender would not even be mentioned at the Olympics – that's what I think.

I believe, sports-women are probably more likely to be open to competing with their male counterparts than the other way around. Maybe the woman hasn't been pushed enough and fully tested, and could come out tops if she is. It could just be a psychological barrier and not necessarily a physical one. We just don't know. Male chauvinists may refuse to play against females, or even if they did, they may not put in their 100% – maybe they'd feel insecure that it could have a Roger Bannister effect. It's all too complicated; just remove the gender bias!

A Tanka:

Cheechu is a cat
like any other feline
but a bit different
he's naughty, cute and wise with
the softest fluff in the world

Where and how we are right now is the result of everything that has happened to us right up to this very moment, plus the way we've responded to those experiences. Our current level of abundance, physical or metaphysical, is largely due to our past thoughts, experiences, environment, actions and perspectives.

So if you'd like your future, short or long term, to be better and more fulfilling, then your present has to be filled with more open-mindedness, flexibility and inclusiveness; and whatever you do, do it with devotion, purpose and intent.

Every night we die, to take birth in the morning.

You may be thinking that I don't really embody or live everything I'm saying. You're right, I probably don't, but I do try to incorporate, as much as possible, all the intellectual understanding I've gained on this journey into the way I function. Furthermore, how would you know if any of the famous teachers or gurus you're following are living and breathing 24/7 what they say? Please don't go by their nice behaviour, kind gestures or least of all their polite words, because none of that really matters in comparison to how they truly *are*. Even if they are living it 24/7, which I very much doubt, why do I have to? Just take me for a coach, who's only imparting the knowledge and understanding. There's enough evidence in the sporting world – of excellent coaches who were never really "excellent" at the sport themselves.

A few years into enquiry, I got severely stuck in a phase of *maya* and the illusory nature of everything. Not mere imagining, but reality itself seemed an illusion. Every time I looked up at the sky, the moon, the sun and stars, I would get drawn into a sort of void and deeply deliberate about the what-is-all-this-ness.

Much later I learnt, through an epiphany, that everything is actually real. The grandness of the universe and its intelligence is reality. All of space and time and their contents, including planets, stars, galaxies, and all other forms of matter and energy is really real. Your existence, and the experiencing of the grandness of this non-stop movement of everything, that goes on and on with precision and intention is all true reality. You ignoring all this magic and magnificence of the cosmos, and making the infinitesimally small "I" more important is the illusion. The ignorance of your ignorance is ignorance.

Maya is our unawareness, our obliviousness and our trivial pursuits. The notion that our perspectives, beliefs, obligations, commitments, and base thoughts and emotions are all real, is the illusion.

Here I am

But you're saying I am not the body

That's right

You're also saying that I am not the mind

True

And you're also saying that I'm not all the senses?

Correct

Then what am I, nothing?

The "confidence" that is raved about in today's world is suffused with close-mindedness – it is exclusive rather than inclusive. I remember many years ago when I used to work with a financial institution, I was told by a quality analyst to always speak with confidence, even if I were providing the wrong answer. Funny, right?! I come across some "confident" people who are really insecure – they're always trying to mask or hide their incompetence by the way they walk and talk. And when they make a mistake they just laugh it off rather than own it. There are other "confident" people who have a sense of always being right and are constantly trying to defend, justify or prove their way, and rubbish and belittle other perspectives. Such people always like to have the last word, not realising that the true confident person will have the last word – through silence. After all, speech is only silver.

Anyways, the characteristics of this "confidence", quite accepted in the western world, are selfishness, one-upmanship, arrogance, and even mild sarcasm or condescension when pushed into a corner. All of this boils down to one thing – the 4-letter word that starts with F. I'm not saying that the true confident person is not fearful, it's just that they understand that fear inherently is part of the everyday life of survival, and it is important to include both fear and courage into their *being*. The truly confident person is open-minded and inclined to learning, they're better listeners, appreciate the not-knowing of something and aren't ashamed to admit it. They don't need to look up to anyone, nor do they need to disrespect, disregard or look down upon anyone.

You know what you know, you know what you don't know. But you don't even know what you don't know!

With everything being said about multitasking, I say, at least avoid doing anything else when you're eating. Just eat while you're eating.

Don't let any other activity – watching TV, being on your phone, reading a book, or even thinking – get in the way of you and your food. Just be with and enjoy your food. Don't even speak while you're eating, at the very least when you have food in your mouth and you're chewing. How can you allow thoughts to come to you while your entire focus should be on relishing the food you're chewing?

By the way, I didn't write this piece while having my breakfast… :-)

Not sure what happened, but that beautiful sensation I had in my body completely went away in December 2017. I kept thinking it'll come back, after having had it for more than 5 years. Alas, it was gone. It may have started sometime in mid-2012 when I first made my foray into enquiry. As I delved deeper into introspecting the self, and was having several awakening experiences, that sensation strengthened and became more ecstatic. I had fully gotten used to having it, and in fact it peaked in 2016 and 2017.

It was a euphoric kind of sensation. I've never been able to express or explain it properly, but it was one of pleasantness and bliss on a cellular or maybe even atomic level. The months that followed its going away, I was depressed. I felt heavy-hearted, so down-hearted and altogether broken-hearted. I quit my job, hinting that I wanted to become a recluse, a sage. I didn't do anything for a few months, then took up another job with a leading bank, which I also left after two months. Mentally I had hit a low, with frustration being at the very core of it. But thanks to a few distractions like *carnatic* music, my new Bullet 350 and Netflix, not to mention my ever-supportive wife, daughter and cat, I was able to somehow get over that low period.

I still cannot articulate that beautiful sensation I had in my body. Boy, what I wouldn't give to reacquire that.

Cheechu,

Thank you for choosing us and this house. You are complete and utter love. You are beauty and you bring joy to the world just with your presence. Everything you do fills our hearts with joy and immense love, even your just sitting still or sleeping signifies present-moment awareness and consciousness. We thank you for looking after yourself in all aspects – mind, body, emotion and spirit. You are Tac in cat form made to perfection.

Is there such a thing as time? What is past, present and future? There is only the present, a never-ending now which we can experience but never get a hold of. Now is an experience of the present moment. A happening is an event of the past, something that has already happened. We can interpret and judge the event but it cannot be changed. Now is the consequence of past occurrences, and the unknown future is the consequence of past and the present. Everything I've written until now is already in the past. And the now is over even before we think about it, and becomes the past.

Now is a moment that is always moving, never constant. The past is etched only in our memories and the future hasn't taken shape yet although it is determined by the past and present. So if every present moment is always moving into the future which is constantly becoming the past, what is the present? Is there a now? Even if it's there, how do we define it? Maybe that's the 13-letter word that starts with C!

It tends to not be about what's being said, but who's saying it. Why is it that the bearer is more important than the content itself? What I mean is, all these things I say, no matter how sincere or prudent, or no matter how well it's iterated, holds no credibility and won't be heeded. Why? Because I'm not a celebrity personal development teacher, a mystic or a famous guru. If someone like fill-in-the-blank said the very same things, then that would be revered and put on a pedestal. It's like the attention musical compositions and songs, books, art, photographs and films, or even food get – it's sad that the content or the product doesn't hold for much, no matter how good it is, unless there's a name or brand attached to it. That's just how it is. It is unfortunate that I need to get approval from the celebrity-crazed world before anything a "nobody" such as me says is taken note of. Not that I'm particularly looking for any kind of validation for the things I say.

When you've got nothing to lose, you give it everything. It's like when you cannot go any further down, then the only way is up.

We've seen this happening a lot in a tennis match, especially at the "business end" of a tournament. When a good player is down and almost out, they start to dig deeper, take more risks and suddenly the momentum shifts; many times they end up winning the match.

We're always seeking success. Even when it comes to doing the littlest of things, like pouring yourself a glass of water or throwing something in the trash, you want to do it successfully. That being said, the words failure and success are like two sides of the same coin; both are basically outcomes or results. The former is not in alignment with our desires or goals, and the latter is. Failure is an outcome that represents how we may have neglected to be disciplined and focussed, lacked in determination and not having taken appropriate action at the right time.

So how can we avoid failure and achieve success? By consistently practising fundamentals, managing time well, not getting distracted, overcoming the ridicule of others and of the self, and consistently moving forward.

You're right. I may be saying that I'm not looking to justify or prove anything to anyone, and that there are no bottom lines, but let me contradict myself and say that there may be a few bottom lines: a) everything is consciousness, b) there's no real purpose to life, c) it is possible to understand and experience reality, and d) what you're directly experiencing is the only reality.

"Each to their own" or "whatever floats your boat" are some of the most obtuse and irresponsible comments I hear when I talk about raising consciousness. Agreed, you have a right to personal preferences and opinions, but you're not totally free to do anything you want. That's why there are laws, rules and regulations, right?

I believe I am equally part of the community and society and have as much entitlement, as the government and legislators, to suggest how we function and live as good samaritans. Raising individual and collective consciousness is the most important thing, in fact it's the only thing for us to pursue. There's nothing else! All red herrings like your work, business, friends, family, hobbies and other interests are all there to take us towards the ultimate goal: to get enlightened and totally understand reality. Yet, we're totally unconscious and in denial about this, and just don't take any responsibility towards enriching our awareness.

Love can only be given. If there's only you in your world, then love has to stem from you – how can you expect it to come to you? For that matter, even happiness and other emotions – positive or negative – have to emanate from you. You are the giver. You may say, "how much can you just keep giving, don't they have any responsibility?" I say that that's *their* choice, and it has to stem from them. How can you coerce them to love you? What you can do is be in a state of love, happiness and openness. Nothing, especially from outside, should be able to overpower that state of yours.

Meditate like you're dead. When you meditate in a state of no mind, no body, no senses, then there's only you as consciousness itself.

Isn't it obvious why you have two ears but only one mouth? To listen twice as much as you speak! Get ready for my rant.

Almost all of us are all about ourselves, constantly seeking attention and suffering from a condition called verbal diarrhoea – words (sounds) keep flowing out of our mouths incessantly. We're just not interested in listening or asking questions. We think we know everything, and have absolutely no sense of curiosity to increase knowledge. If any of such people happen to hold a big degree from a university, or a senior position in any organisation, or if they're just the intellectual type, then the most you'll get out of them is something like "how's work?" Ha. Then there are those who like to be judged as "cool" and just won't talk, unless you ask them a question. These pinheads will go to gatherings and parties but will stay aloof and not really socialise. Wonder why we even encourage such behaviour. I can put this all down to just one thing: insecurity.

If death is the ultimate orgasm, then life has to be foreplay. And the quality of the orgasm is dependent upon the quality of the foreplay. So then the question is: how do you have a great foreplay (or life)?

First of all you have to be a romantic. You have to be adventurous and passionate at your very core, which means you have to incorporate variety in what you do. You have to try doing different things in life, at the very least vocationally. You can't stick to one job or profession and do that for your entire life. Please don't ask what's wrong with that; ask what's right, then contemplate. Another thing is to move cities or countries every few years.

Understand that you don't have any responsibilities towards anyone other than yourself, and the more integrity you have with yourself, the more it will automatically outpour to all your relationships and interactions, whether that's with family members, coworkers, friends or even strangers. A full and meaningful life is one that has more and varied experiences in it, not one that involves doing the same thing in the same place for 40 or 50 years and then preparing to lie on the deathbed – metaphorical or otherwise.

"I can't breathe". The racial crisis that's been ongoing for centuries, especially white vs black, will continue to exist as long as the media, movies and culture keep presenting all the discrimination in one way or another. Even the white person apologising or feeling remorse, or making documentaries and movies about slavery and oppression, or presenting themselves as the devil, is all a discreet projection of this divide.

Although some incidents have sparked worldwide protests, racism still exists in a big way, not just by usage of slurs but more so subtly and silently. Silent racism cannot be explicitly seen or heard but takes place in a way that you cannot clearly pinpoint, which can be as distressing as acts of blatant racism. Having been subjected to racism on many occasions, I find that this form of racism isn't loud or in your face, yet the discrimination is still present, and can be upsetting.

I may sound like a broken record, but any kind of prejudice is low conscious, whether it's based on class, caste, gender, colour or creed. Therefore, it should not be just about the oppressor or the oppressed, but about consciousness and raising it. That's only possible through never-ending self-education, learning and unbiased travelling.

P.S. Many companies and organisations tend to include a variety of races only to appear multicultural and diverse.

I'm getting a few ideas for the title of this book:
No Bottom Lines
Not Another Indian Guru
Introspections
Contemplations
Soliloquy
Frustrations
Vichāras
Deliberations
Acquiescence
Contradictions
Bildungsroman

As for the format of this book, I got the inspiration from a book by Marcus Aurelius called *Meditations*.

There was a time, actually a significantly long period when I took myself off socialising and mingling with people, or even just ringing them – Covid-19 isolation excluded. I also went off all the popular social media apps, and used my phone only for the odd call or text message, or to listen to music or podcasts. I removed voicemail services too. I wouldn't say that I had become a misanthrope, but my interest in chit-chatting and having casual conversations really ran down.

My world revolved only around my wife and daughter – who seemed to understand almost everything I was going through or saying – but more importantly, around myself. And I didn't mind people judging me how ever they wanted, for mind you, I was definitely judging them big time! Not necessarily as right/wrong or good/bad, but trying to discern them. Many took offence, which didn't bother me – for it was not my problem but their very own. If they couldn't understand or appreciate my philosophy or state of mind with inclusiveness, then that's only because of their own lack of open-mindedness, and their inability to accept situations and people unconditionally. As for me, I didn't have a problem with anyone, it's just that the phase I was in was of frustration and confusion, that demanded self-integrity and solitude, and if I didn't heed to that, then I would be disregarding the most important person in my life: me.

Having spent almost the entire last decade trying to raise my consciousness, I have certain values and principles I live by and if people violate them, it's only reasonable for me to carve them out. If you're looking to give this condition a psychological or medical term like social anxiety, midlife crisis or whatever, that's again your choice – but bear in mind that it only speaks about your own judgemental and dogmatic ways, and your self-biases.

I'm probably still in that phase, and may or may not come out of it, but either way, I don't mind whether I'm accepted or not for how I am or will be.

Maybe I am, on a subconscious level, de-spirited about not getting the attention from people – that they're not interested in any of the epistemic research and enquiry I was or am still doing about existence, life, truth, self, reality and consciousness.

One of the first things I experimented with when I got into this journey was taking cold showers every morning. It was basically a response to a thought that occurred to me one Melbourne winter morning, and since "I couldn't afford the luxury of a negative thought – not even one", I decided to give it a shot. I must say, it was one of the most radical things I had done and I couldn't believe I did it. At that point, I didn't think or know of any of its health benefits but I was just being instinctive and courageous, and following my curiosity. And I still do it.

P.S. Look up Wim Hof.

I have enough inadequacies. Me saying all these things doesn't mean that I have mastery over my emotions and easily navigate through life. No. I probably suffer and face more challenges than most others, because of how sensitive, intuitive and judgemental I've become of everything and everyone, including myself. As much as I see deficiencies without, I also see them within. And I point them out, no matter where or in whom I see them, even in myself. I'm not playing victim here or trying to be humble, I'm just being real. That's the beauty of this work; as much as I judge and criticise others, I do the same, if not more, to myself.

Your current employees are your biggest assets! Why do you not get this?! When someone new joins your organisation, you do everything to show how well you look after your employees, but it's more important to display that care and concern to your *existing* staff. These are the people who've been getting up every morning to come to work for you. Agreed, they may be doing it for themselves, but they don't turn up elsewhere.

Most organisations only like to talk about their integrity towards their employees via slogans and taglines without fully living the slogans themselves. After all, an organisation is only a concept, a story, but it's the people that make that story.

There's only one thing. For how long you make it your magnificent obsession is the question.

Here we are. Not even sure a) how we got here, b) if we even had a choice to get here, c) what is it that we are, and d) what this thing called life is.

Anyways, here we are. Surrendering ourselves to the people around us – parents, siblings, grandparents, society, friends, teachers, school and media. We trust that they're all helping us live an abundant, meaningful and purposeful life, without realising that we're basically letting ourselves be conditioned by whatever they've been conditioned to. So it's conditioning over conditioning over conditioning hundredfold or thousandfold going right back to the early evolution of humanity. But is the only reason we're here, to somehow get through infancy to childhood, to adolescence to adulthood, whilst going through whatever the majority consider "education"? Just so that we can have a career which would last until "retirement" and then wait for the eventuality?

Your vocabulary changes. That's one of the biggest changes you will notice in yourself when you're introspecting and doing self-enquiry. The bulk of your language will centre around words like consciousness, reality, the self, truth, love, ego, inclusiveness, awakening, spirituality, illusion, science, yoga, nature and joy. However, everywhere you go, the language you'll hear from most people is quite the opposite – completely devoid of any of the aforementioned words.

When you take on this path of self-enquiry, you basically give up that old language for new words and expressions. Having taken on a new identity, you not only stop using those mundane words, but even avoid listening to them. You will either choose silence, or remove yourself from situations where the language you hear doesn't resonate with you.

From a dietary point of view, it's good to, every once in a while, stretch your mind and body towards extremity. I'm hinting at fasting. We live too much in and around balance, or maintaining it all the time, whether it be room temperature or food or exercise or sleep. Stretching outside your comfort zone sends a message to the body and mind about the full extent of your range of possibilities and abilities. Do you always only consume room temperature drinks? Probably not – you may have a cup of hot beverage at one time, and an iced drink at another. And for food, you either eat the right amount or overfill yourself.

This is where fasting comes in – it's equally important to go the other direction. It's okay to bring a bit of suffering into your life – consciously and with awareness. As you're doing that, observe, notice and introspect the happenings within your physiology and psychology. I could suggest water fasting, even if done for 12 or 24 hours on a regular basis (weekly or fortnightly) as a tremendous way to boost one's ability to stretch.

The moment someone is *diagnosed* with a medical condition, they start to get all the care, attention and compassion from everywhere. Not to mention, that all these conditions have a name and a label, and everyone reacts more to the label and the prognosis than to the condition itself. It's the labelling and the prognosis that are the issues here. What was just a condition for many years/decades has today been given a particular tag or identity. That's why I think that prognoses don't hold much water, as they're mere statistics and too objective, whereas both illness and wellness have a very large component of subjectivity in them.

"We just have to live it, what's the alternative?" Is there a purpose to life?! Is there a reason we've taken birth? My answer at this point is that I'm not fully convinced there's a purpose or reason to life – of any life form for that matter. I believe we're just part of this thing called evolution. If we stripped away everything that we think we are, and everything we sense i.e. see, hear, touch, smell and taste, and viewed everything from the perspective of the universe or cosmos, then we will understand that we and all forms of life are just products of evolution.

Did the creator or the divine intelligence or truth or god or infinity really create us and all forms of life for a reason? As much as most of us would like to think in the affirmative, I'm not entirely sure about that. It is us that gives everything meaning, by labelling and identifying everything through our own thoughts, perspectives and words. Some of the biggest labels we give ourselves are nationality, gender and name – not to mention that we even call ourselves human beings. The reason we like to talk about purpose is only because it can make our lives more interesting and more experiential. Also because at a deeper, almost unconscious level, we do understand that there isn't a purpose of life, yet we still must go through it – so we'd rather give it a meaning than not. If we're all just part of evolution, and there's no purpose to life, it surely doesn't mean that you can now be obnoxious, and give up on everything. Not at all, if you understand what I mean, then you have to now double-down on whatever you think is meaningful for you to pursue, to live a full-fledged life – go after it with purpose and devotion.

I may always be talking about not sticking to any ideology, belief or doctrine but a lot of what I am discussing is on the lines of Jainism, Taoism and Stoicism, and maybe even Solipsism.

Biodiversity is the variety and quantity of all life on Earth, and includes everything from tiny microbes, insects and plants to blue whales, animals and forests. Conserving and protecting biodiversity is the key, and is probably the best answer to global warming and climate change. And biodiversity is seriously shrinking, due to the combined actions of our everyday life choices. Most of us don't actively try to harm nature or reduce biodiversity, but what we do each day, no matter how small, is possibly contributing towards habitat loss.

With conscious awareness and some simple practices, we can lessen our own adverse environmental impact on biodiversity – stopping usage of plastic bags, reducing the use of pesticides and fertilisers, planting trees, growing wildlife-friendly gardens and patios, avoiding walking on grass, reducing, reusing and recycling with an emphasis on *reducing*, practising minimalism, having less children, buying less meat and dairy, buying sustainably harvested seafood, reducing food wastage, reducing electricity and water usage at home and at work, and turning off your car engine when not needed.

"You never see everything that I'm doing well, but you're quick to point out whenever I err". Absolutely, that's how everything works. We're meant to always be good and do the right things, and if we don't, it will be pointed out to us. Does the law or government or even your manager reward you every time you do the right thing? No, but they will book or question you if you didn't.

Find comfort in discomfort.

Back when I was in my phase of "balance", I started to experiment with doing certain things with my non-dominant hand. Things like: brushing teeth, shaving, using the computer mouse, wearing my watch or belt, eating and writing. Just so I could reduce imbalances, expand my comfort zone, not do things mindlessly, and also become more open-minded and creative. I did overdo it for some time, but now I have a more balanced way: left days and right days – odd dates are left, even days right.

Everything that I'm stating here is the outcome of having learnt, experimented, researched and contemplated about hundreds of topics and situations. That's the thing about epistemology, the philosophical study of the origin and nature of knowledge – it's a never-ending journey without a destination.

I'm thankful to Dr David Hawkins for acquainting me with Kinesiology, a form of therapy that uses muscle monitoring to look at imbalances that may be causing discomfort and dis-ease in the body.

Kinesiology is one of the most holistic of natural therapies, wherein the body's own energy is used to bring a state of balance within one's body. Every thought and feeling we have somehow manifests in physical form in our own physiology, and what better way to spread that understanding than through Kinesiology? Muscle-testing is used to detect the underlying cause of discomfort and then suitable corrective measures are provided to remedy the cause.

P.S. I completed the course in late 2015 and have been experimenting with it immensely, to solidify my understanding of consciousness.

Trust your instincts and follow your intuitions only *after* you have spent enough time in introspection, contemplation and enquiry.

Only such abuse that is *obvious* is reported, like physical or verbal abuse. What about emotional abuse? It's hardly talked about. Domestic or societal violence is not limited to physical or verbal abuse alone; emotional abuse can be just as destructive, if not more damaging, and can severely impact mental health. The scars of emotional abuse can be real and last for a very long time. Besides having a negative impact on one's self-esteem and confidence, emotional abuse can leave them feeling anxious, depressed or disconnected from their Self.

Mild emotional abuse can involve things like rejecting opinions, sarcasm, gaslighting, condescension or putting one down. More serious emotional abuse like bullying can involve making one feel afraid, intimidated or threatened, which can limit one's freedom in different ways.

There was a gathering organised for a group of yogis, monks and sages. It was organised by academicians, professors and other intellectuals who wanted to get the group's perspective on concepts like consciousness, self and reality. At the gathering, it so happened that only the intellectuals discussed all those topics with intensity and vigour. The yogis and the mystics just sat there perplexed, listening to everything that was vehemently being discussed. Every now and then the group was asked questions, however, due to the lack of vocabulary to effectively articulate the responses, they were mostly left unanswered.

To a degree, we all have our own biases and prejudices – whether that's towards countries, ethnicities, religions, races or even towards certain ideologies, philosophies and perspectives. And the only way we can transcend any such biases or prejudices is by becoming more aware, more conscious and spiritually-evolved.

Let's first understand that doing any kind of consciousness work is completely independent of our background. Also, that we don't necessarily need to fulfil basic survival needs before starting to make any spiritual progress. Go to a country like India and visit Kashi (Varanasi or Benares) and you'll see what I mean. It's very hard for much of the western world or the intellectual mind – that carries out any investigation using logic, analysis and dissection – to fully comprehend what is being said here. Intellectualism will hardly help when it comes to investigating the Self, reality, Truth or consciousness. I'm not totally undermining the importance of intellectual knowledge, but going within has to be the starting point. And as you pursue this investigation with sincerity you will become less prejudiced and biased.

"You really have the audacity to talk about biases and prejudices when you hail from India, a country steeped in its caste system?!" Well, do you even hear yourself? You are suffering from a condition called myopia, and don't even know you have it! It's not something an optometrist can treat. What kind of understanding do you have about the system? How many hours of research have you conducted on the caste system? How many books on the system have you read? Actually, how many books have you read?

Look, I'm not condoning or condemning the system, but only stating that it exists, and like anything else it too has evolved. How it functions and is perceived today is probably very different to when it began. I'm sure you'd agree that such hierarchy-based systems exist in (almost) every part of the world, regardless of how "developed" the country is or not, and prejudice abounds everywhere. Only by devoting yourself to consciousness work can you get over any such preconceived notions.

The Greek word Cosmos means
order, arrangement, and harmony.

"I am confident, I am courageous, I am disciplined". That's the very first affirmation I came up with, barely a few weeks into this journey. And I recall affirming it every morning for months, and the results were evident.

What are affirmations and how do they work? They're verbal statements, in the present tense, that are designed to reprogram the subconscious mind and create change within the individual who does them routinely. The idea is to recite these sentences continuously for long periods of time, as a routine, so that you're able to go beyond the words, beyond the thoughts, and even beyond the feelings – and you actually *become* that very affirmation.

Most of the time we're subconsciously doing negative affirmations, without even knowing we're doing them. Positive affirmations, on the other hand, are basically words we vocally recite in order to nullify those silent negative ones. The best time to do them is upon waking up. Trust me, it is a highly effective tool to bring about self-change, and you can see results fairly quickly.

The unawakened dreams, while the awakened is busy going about realising their dreams. To awaken spiritually is to awaken mentally and physically.

If I had one wish then it would be for everyone to experience what I have experienced. I'm not bragging, but please understand that there's nothing else, absolutely nothing else more meaningful and wonderful in life than to experience an awakening to non-duality – that everything is you and you everything.

Many times in the first few years of this journey I'd be overwhelmed with tears of joy and love, and constantly ask myself: "why me, why now?" And this happened a lot for the first 3–4 years – just looking at trees, moon, stars and the rising sun would move me to tears. There was also a nice sensation in my body that lasted for a few years. While all this was happening, I didn't need to give up on my "normal" life – whether that be playing or following sport, doing my job, pursuing money, being a family man, socialising or interacting with people. As much as I was living a philosophical and contemplative life – like a hermit or a sage – I didn't have to forego much. Obviously now I'm in a different phase on this odyssey, as you can gather from my content.

Immortal is *I'm mortal*.

"Look at me!" Attention-seeking is a condition a lot of us suffer from. Much of what we do is less for ourselves and more for the adulation and accolades of others. Filmstars, musicians, media persons and politicians are probably some of the obvious ones always looking to get attention, but even some personal development teachers and spiritual gurus do the same. What I feel highly concerned about though is the current generation of young people, who identify or measure success by only numbers on social media – as in likes, views, comments or subscribers – and therefore continually find the need to get approval from their followers. Whilst these numbers provide some encouragement, too much dependence upon them or craving for them can make it an obsession or even a bad addiction. The sooner they're able to emotionally mature and fill up any void or inner emptiness, the lesser they'll need to look for external validation. And it all starts by grounding oneself in solitude and working on the inner self – through reading, writing in a journal, exercising, eating healthy, meditation, and perhaps most importantly, reducing all screen time.

What we're seeking is holistic wealth and success, which only ensues as a byproduct of our effort, devotion and personal philosophy. We cannot have an external life any better than our internal one.

Broadly speaking, there are only 5 "external" areas we're always looking to enhance and develop viz. health, finance, relationships, career and recreation. Although health, to a very large extent, is an external aspect, a big part of good health is dependent upon your mental attitude and awareness. Finance and career are separate facets and may not necessarily be related to each other. And by relationships, I don't only mean the connection with family and friends, but also with workmates, strangers, pets and with Mother Earth and her biodiversity. Last but not least, we are sensory beings, and sport, adventure, travel and pursuing hobbies do contribute towards us leading a full and holistic life.

How would an ideal day look like for you? Try writing down everything you'd like to include in your ideal day. It'll give you perspective.

When you're counting blessings or doing your gratitude affirmations, note that the sentences or words that you use don't matter – they're only a tool, a vehicle you're using in order to get into a state of gratitude. That very state of *being* is what you're after.

Unless you go beyond the words, thoughts and feelings you're wasting your time doing the affirmations. Come to think of it, there are people who repeat Sanskrit mantras without actually knowing the meaning, but their belief in the mantras is so positive and strong that they reap the benefits. Essentially, what I'm trying to say is that the devotion and intensity you put into doing the affirmations, combined with your inner or mental vision is what creates the magic, not the thoughtless mumbling of words.

I haven't personally met anyone who's actually *wise*, in the truest sense of the word – who's awake, who has the awareness about consciousness and the nature of reality, and of life. I'm not implying I'm any of that, but having researched and deliberated upon wakefulness for so many years, I have a fairly decent understanding of what true wisdom is – even if that understanding is only from an intellectual point of view.

Some of the things I've been doing in this process of waking up:

Journaling – writing down a stream of consciousness regularly.

Working out everyday – physically and mentally: running, swimming, cycling, playing sport or doing basic *hatha yoga*.

Playing brain games on some popular apps, and doing sudoku and crosswords – cryptic and regular.

Completing the Competent Communicator Program in Toastmasters.

Learning and teaching Carnatic music.

Re-learning advanced mathematics.

Learning Portuguese.

Spending time in solitude – easily one of the best ways to contemplate upon the true nature of reality and the Self.

Alternating usage of left and right hands – brushing teeth, shaving, mouse usage, eating and drinking.

Enrolling in a Life coaching course.

Eating a different breakfast every morning.

Reading a variety of books, mainly non-fictional.

Writing down a gratitude list and counting blessings.

Learning *tai chi*.

Using positive language and expressions, and consciously avoiding negative words and complaining.

Having a cold shower at least once every day.

Completing a course in Kinesiology.

Rideshare driving.

Laughing first thing every morning.

Doing affirmations – words can be powerful if used properly.

Practising visualisation techniques.

Practising different kinds of meditation.

Practising minimalism.

Getting up early, and heading out on a solo walk.

Eating mainly a plant-based diet.

Following a financial plan.

Pursuing hobbies – music, sport, games.

Frequently travelling and going away on holidays.

Nurturing relationships with animals and birds, plants and trees.

Volunteering and serving.

If we can trust our body and immune system to quickly heal a tiny cut on our finger, why can't we trust it for other medical conditions?

Are people envious of me? Is that why they stay away?

Because I have broken free from societal pressures, and have taken the path most have only heard or read about?

Because I've had awakening and mystical experiences, and have got some understanding about the self, truth and reality?

Because I'm able to bask in the beauty of solitude, when many have various insecurities and worries that they have to always be in the company of other insecure and worried people?

Because unlike pragmatic people, I'm committed to growing and developing the one *most* important relationship?

Because I'm fully committed to continuous learning and education?

Because I don't have much on "the list of things that I'm unwilling to be, do and have"?

Or is it because I'm not seeking any kind of validation for anything from anyone?

Leadership means to be in control of others, right?! Many will agree. And even the few who don't may not fully understand and practise everything that's inherent to true leadership – most of all that it has nothing to do with a designation, position or title.

Leadership is actually a behaviour, a set of specific skills, a mental attitude, none of which most "leaders" possess or are willing to work on. It's frustrating to see some supervisors, team leaders and managers without any people-skills use bullying tactics and behave with sheer idiocy merely because of some "title" they hold. They're nothing but tyrants, maybe not like the names that immediately come to mind, but definitely are a milder version.

Even if you don't consider yourself as one of them, my question to you is: how consistently are you a true leader? It's easy for anyone to be a good leader when things are going well. How do you lead or respond when the rug's been pulled from under you? Of course you'll say you're consistent!

When you're truly spiritual or conscious, you are automatically in a mode of happiness, gratitude, goodness, enthusiasm, inspiration, love, humility, trust, authenticity, detachment and inclusiveness. However, this may not be visibly seen by the general masses; in fact it can quite easily be misinterpreted – as everything *but* all of the above.

Try eliminating the concept of your own birth and even death; *this here right now* is all there is. This. Here. Now. The present moment can never be grasped for it's in flux, always in motion, yet the only Truth. This here now is reality. You could capture it in a photograph, which can be seen, albeit in the future, but not fully experienced through all your senses.

Well-rounded – *adjective* – (of a person) having a personality that is fully developed in all aspects.

That's pretty much the opposite of a square person. A well rounded person is one who functions easily, efficiently and effortlessly regardless of the situation they're in, or what or whom they're dealing with. It's like the wheels of a bike or car, they don't have to be round, but to function smoothly at maximum efficiency and with least amount of friction, they're made round.

We're all on the same path, and by *we* I mean not just humans but every living being. On the one hand, we're looking to have, do and become more, but on the other, we're also seeking liberation, *mukti* and *moksha*.

Figuratively speaking, we want to escape the gravitational pull of Earth and simply float in space. But to get there, we need a good deal of rocket fuel to not just break through the atmosphere, but to even just liftoff. And all the multitude of situations, people and experiences we face day in and out is the rocket fuel in this metaphor. The gurus and masters that come on our path are to provide us the ignition to propel us off the ground and to sustain it.

Look, you have to truly want this – to fully awaken and become self-aware. You have to go through all the introspection and enquiry, and ask question after question, looking for answers and bottom lines that are black and white and concrete; until you get to a point when you realise that there are only questions, and no real answers. And as you keep soldiering on, you will eventually get to a place of only being in awe. That place of no questions, no answers, just *being*.

Much of the world only knows about the relative good and evil, the relative truth and falsehood, the relative love and fear, the relative right and wrong. But above all these dualities lie only one Goodness, one Truth, one Love, one Reality.

Relatively speaking, even the largest organised religions are a fairly new concept. Although humans have been around for hundreds of thousands of years, Buddhism is only about two and a half thousand years old, Christianity about two thousand, and Islam only about one and a half thousand. They really didn't start spreading worldwide until only about a few hundred years ago with the emergence of sea travel.

If you carefully see, the organised religions are all competing with each other, they're about one-upmanship and have more prejudices, bigger egos and separating abilities than even political boundaries. Now, even if you're an atheist or intellectual, please don't consider yourself "above" the religious fundamentalists, because sticking to any belief and being rigid is in itself dogma or even bigotry. All said, it's only a matter of time before more and more people realise all the brainwashing and indoctrination they've been subjected to for so long, all in the name of god and religion.

I don't consider myself from any country. I may hail from a region that the world calls India, but I say: "no place is home, every place is home". Whilst I don't have any particular affinity to any country, I don't have any kind of aversion to any either. I wish we were all more "patriotic", than overly nationalistic. Although both are just linguistic expressions, I feel there's more inclusiveness in patriotism. And because of all the infrastructural and technological development that's happening, the world's "becoming smaller" and more accessible to everyone; and nationalistic and political ideologies and movements that are more extreme and exclusionary become unsustainable. By patriotism I mean that you love your country, but not any more than any other country, or conversely, that you love any other country as your own.

One of the biggest gripes I have about people is, not that they don't ask questions, but that they often don't even allow me to ask them questions. They talk so incessantly that I can't even fit in a question. It's shocking to see how deluded some people are, especially when I see them having conversations. Everyone is talking, laughing, complaining, all at the same time, and I'm standing there absolutely nonplussed. I sometimes wonder how I manage to put myself in such situations to see all this?

You were born, and thus began the never-ending process of responding. The body responds to everything you give, feed or do to it. As good health and wellness is a response of your body, so is sickness and ill-health. Out-breath is the response of the in-breath and vice versa. Things happen, and we respond. In a subtle way we're constantly responding to experiences – in a fight, flight or freeze mode i.e. by changing, leaving or accepting the experience.

It was 12th November 2013, roughly 20 months into this odyssey, when I had a sort of a mystical experience. On this morning, as I was outside doing *surya namaskar*, I had a vision of Jesus Christ, Krishna, Prophet Mohammad and Gautama Buddha. They were standing in front of me with their arms around each other's shoulders, like they were a clique. It seemed quite real, and it probably had a lot to do with the kind of books I was reading at the time. Upon deliberating and contemplating the episode, I concluded that a) these spiritual masters were just people like you and me, of flesh and bones and mind, who after spending enough time contemplating the nature of reality, became fully conscious and enlightened; b) they had attained exalted levels of awareness through their own introspection of the self and life; c) they were asking us not to worship them, but to find god within; d) that they themselves had fully surrendered to the infinite intelligence or consciousness or god.

If only the theologians properly interpreted the principles of all religions. They would see that the underlying teachings of each of them are basically the same, whether they be about love or oneness. All this religious separation and prejudice we see have been created by close-minded, myopic and obtuse people, who have manipulated and controlled the majority of humanity that also happens to be close-minded, myopic and obtuse.

Exactly a year later, on 12th November 2014, that experience reoccured as I was returning home from badminton training – all 4 of them were in my car this time.

Learn music, a language or mathematics. And if you can learn any two of the three, or even all three, the benefits are multitudinous.

I've been doing a 1000-second meditation. It's a nice short one to improve mindfulness. I'm either sitting, lying down or even standing up with eyes closed near a clock, and I count every alternate ticking of the second hand. So when I've counted up to 100, it means that I've meditated for 200 seconds. And I do five rounds of it.

I may say a lot of things, even rant and criticise in frustration, but an important aspect of everything I'm suggesting is about being truly happy and enthusiastic, as in *joie de vivre, eudaimonia* or *ananda*. It's not the kind that almost all of humanity considers happiness i.e. the conditional one, but the opposite kind. And that's the root cause of all my exasperation – I don't see much unconditional happiness anywhere, and everyone seems to be on some sort of treadmill chasing base pleasure, entertainment or some frivolous enjoyment, not realising that what they're actually seeking is liberation or *moksha*.

Your body is constantly working. Even when you're sleeping it's working, ensuring all your organs function properly. You always take a break from work or any other activity, and it's only obvious that your body deserves breaks as well. Being still, not moving any of your joints, fasting for a few hours or skipping a couple of meals every few days, can all help your body get the much-needed break.

There are businesses, organisations and even restaurants that ask for feedback once they've completed providing their services to you. The following is a rant, after I was subjected to an appalling service from a business, who then had the audacity to ask me for feedback.

Why should I provide them feedback? Why can't they figure it out for themselves? I have spent years, so much effort, time and money in educating myself through reading, journaling, listening to audiobooks and podcasts, doing courses, contemplating, introspecting – all to raise my own consciousness, awareness, knowledge and understanding about different aspects including running a business, customer service, and leadership; and these businesses want to know about all that via a simple feedback! Sorry. Actually, I would kick myself if they just instantly "got it" with my feedback.

Anyways, I don't expect most businesses to act on all the feedback they receive. It would require a radical change in the mindset and attitude of their staff, and a proper overhaul in the philosophy of running the business. Honestly, most of it is not fixable, and could take years if not decades for businesses to understand the whole concept of "customer service" in the true sense. Some organisations would even offer you a refund or compensation, to show that they have resolved your issues; so that they can continue providing the same service (or the lack of it) to their other customers.

Like everyone else, I have my own difficulties and struggles, and each of us has our own way to deal with and resolve them. I'm no guru to give any advice. You could listen to and take suggestions, but then only *you* can execute and apply them to yourself. Only you can live 'em.

Almost everyone has some or the other sickness, pain or suffering (physical or psychological) and everyone is, like it or not, dying. Yes, we are the kind that die at some point in time. So, the question is: are we living or are we dying?

Creation is holonic and happening all around us all the time. As time moves, creation is happening. As a matter of fact, time itself is creation at its very best. It is consciousness. Creation happens not just among humans, but equally everywhere, holarchically. In the animal kingdom, in plants, birds, sea creatures, also in the world of language, where we use labels and words to identify, discern and categorise everything.

Even forgiveness has ego, when you take into account the sentence "I forgive you". But, to be in a *state* of forgiveness is totally different, because *being* is not just a momentary thing, it's the very state of how you are.

The medical and pharmaceutical industry is one of the least conscious industries, only because their work is mainly economically-driven. This industry has created more sickness, illnesses and various kinds of medical conditions, all in the name of health, healing and curing. Doctors, medical professionals and governments are all in bed with the pharmaceutical companies, collectively fooling the asleep masses. Come to think of it, the only way the big pharmas can "peddle" their drugs is through doctors and pharmacies, many of whom get easily enticed by the incentives that they're offered. The industry can only survive, not by curing or healing people, but by keeping them dependent upon the medication and keeping them sick, least of all through side-effects.

As more and more people wake up, we will see an increase in the usage of alternative therapies, not to mention realisation that awareness and consciousness is very largely linked to good health and well-being.

A lot of people look at having a child (or two, even three or four) as a must after marriage. They say things like: "that's just what married couples do", "my parents/in-laws are constantly annoying us", "what will society think about us not having children?" or "both me and my partner have siblings, so we'd also like to have a second one". I've even heard people say "oh, she was an accident!" and they laugh, not realising that their negligence, carelessness and a moment of unmindful weakness has resulted in a human being being conceived; one who has to go through an entire life – pursuing happiness, looking after their health, seeking success and pleasure, yet avoiding pain, suffering, failure, sickness, disappointment. Unless of course this child is able to transcend all dualities like good/bad right/wrong, or high/low. Well, what are the chances of that happening?!

Just because we see the majority of animal life only doing survival activities, we assume that absolutely all of animal life is just about survival. Using words like animalistic or feral is demeaning and condescending to animals. We don't know enough to make any kind of assumptions about them. We view the entire non-human life from our own perspective, and judge it as survival. Isn't much of human life all about survival as well? Probably one in a million human beings become highly aware, conscious or enlightened, and the same could apply to the animal kingdom as well. We don't know!

All I'm saying is that there's more to all life than how we perceive and judge it with our own limited understanding. Being open-minded and in a mode of I-don't-know may help us perceive it better.

There is no history, no past and no future, only the present moment, only the now. And there's only you, and your infinite imagination. Everything is *maya* – illusion. Look up at the sky, the stars and the moon and gaze at them carefully, and you will know what I mean. Earth, sun, air, water are all elements, yet who is the one sensing them? Who's the one seeing the light of the sun and feeling its warmth? Who's feeling the touch of the earth, the smell and sound of the wind, and the taste of water? You.

You do it, only you, and you do it all in the present moment.

There's only individual orgasm. Words like heterosexual, lesbian, homosexual, gay, bisexual, queer are nothing more than social constructs and mere labels we use for needless identification. But none of these words mean much, and there's nothing right/wrong or moral/immoral with any of them, for they all relate to excitement and foreplay. At the very fundamental level there's only one word i.e. culmination, and you really don't need anyone for this "gratification". All the aforementioned labelling is done based on what gender you "use" for the stimulation. That's it. The concept of sex is only one aspect of life, at least in the times and age we live in. And just because a certain group of people are attracted to someone of the same gender, they're labelled!

Some religious texts even say that homosexuality is a sin and that it's wrong. From what authority are these texts basing this idea so vehemently and forcefully? These texts are after all using language and words to express the ideas of the creator or god, so how can it even be close to correct? What language does the creator, god, universe, consciousness or the process of evolution speak in, that the interpreter is able to fully understand what is being said? We've got no idea!

Procreation on the other hand is a completely different aspect and has nothing to do with any of the above labels, although from what we understand, can only occur in heterosexual copulation.

Whether it be the Spiral Dynamics model, Maslow's hierarchy of needs, or Hawkins' Map of Consciousness, the one thing we need to fully grasp and embrace, is the fact that each of us is at a different phase in life and at a different level of awareness and understanding. Having said that, it is possible for someone to be on a certain level (e.g. blue in SD model) at one point in time and at another level (red/turquoise) minutes later.

Life is about constantly managing one's own state of mind at each moment. Each of us has a "shadow", and no two people are the same. No one person is more right/wrong or good/bad than another. We're only on different levels of understanding, and playing our part in raising our own and the collective consciousness of the world, consciously or otherwise.

Just got back from a walk. We're moving into spring and I was noticing the wonderful variety of flowers and leaves of different types and colours. Barely a few weeks ago there were no green leaves or colourful flowers. So what brought about the transformation, or rather who organised this change? It's impossible to fully comprehend everything that goes on. It's all holonic.

Did you know that if Earth wasn't on a tilt, we wouldn't have the different seasons, there would be fewer species and organisms and much less biodiversity, even the sun would shine for 12 hours every day everywhere on the planet? As it does on the equinox, the colder cities would probably be spared the bitter winter chills and sweltering summer heat, but it would also be deprived of changing leaves in autumn and the bloom of flowers in spring.

Get your daily DOSE of "feel-good" chemicals.

Dopamine is all about actually doing things and taking action, even if it means baby steps.

Oxytocin is like a bonding chemical and can be developed by interacting with strangers.

Serotonin by practicing gratitude and surrendering control.

Endorphins through stretching and exercise.

Whatever you do, don't become a seeker, don't ever get into personal development, self-enquiry or spirituality! Unless... You're content only scratching the surface of them. Because if you do spend years in full-time contemplation and introspection trying to comprehend reality, existence, mysticism, consciousness and the metaphysical nature of the Self, then be prepared for a rude awakening. For as you go deeper into understanding reality and see people, society, media and businesses through your new set of lenses, you will face frustration after frustration for not being able to comprehend any of that, more so for not being able to articulate that understanding using conventional language and words. You will be misunderstood big time, massive time! In the initial stages of this journey, you will try to talk to people which they probably won't understand; then in the following stages you will have a lot of spiritual arrogance and become condescending, which will further lead you to simply shaking your head in disbelief, and then eventually into silence.

You'll start to give up on society and people, and you'll see asleep, deluded and unaware people everywhere, people who get easily offended and combative, and you will get exasperated and even depressed by your own understanding and perspectives. You will at some point even feel envious and jealous of other people and want to be as asleep as them, just so that you don't have to undergo all this suffering.

You may think that some of my personal views hover around the philosophy of nihilism, especially when I question morality, authority or life having any meaning or purpose. You're probably right. For that matter, I've even considered myself a misanthrope, especially when I see the innate ignorance, even stupidity, that resides within much of humanity. You must be thinking, all this is just more spiritual arrogance. But what do I do?! What can I do when I view and understand things differently, and in contrast to much of humanity? All of us have a different way of understanding things, and if mine is different and outside of the norm, then so be it. If you have a problem with that, then that's your problem, not mine. I cannot help but continue following my instincts and my curiosity to understand reality and to seek Truth.

As I have maintained, everything that you're reading here are not really mine, they're thoughts that have occurred *to* me, and come from the source; I just happen to be the one listening to them, processing them and putting them out.

What did we come with when we were born? What will we take with us when we die? Aren't the answers to both questions the same? Then why do we keep going after material things – stuff we want, but don't really need? The way I see it, all the things we've accumulated, the stuff we've hoarded will laugh at us at our funeral. The more things we hoard the more we will get laughed at by them.

Religion separates, spirituality unites. Religion is collective ego, and spirituality is transcending both collective and individual ego. However, religion, as a vehicle, is an effective tool or a way to take the masses *towards* spirituality, higher awareness and higher consciousness. The ultimate aim of any religion is to take its followers beyond their own religion, although the religious preachers and pupils are not fully aware of this. For instance, if any one religion were able to convert the entire population of the world to its own religion, then the whole world will automatically become spiritual and united.

Religion, a fully man-made concept of labels, is an attempt at linking the grand intelligence or creator with a name. Spirituality on the other hand is unprejudiced and neutral, helping everyone make conscious contact and merge with that grand intelligence or creator. This intelligence or power is something that has evolved from within, and is merely an experiencing of that connection, yet the religious fundamentalists give credit to what they call Allah, Jesus, Krishna, Rama, Buddha etc.

Evolutionary memory is that you will only get a mango tree when you plant a mango seed, as you'll never get a peach tree from an apple seed.

In spite of all the continuous bombardment of low consciousness and "asleepness" that hits me day in and day out, I'm shocked at myself that I still get shocked at all that. Not that I'm expressively acting out my reactions all the time, but I am always fighting them within and having to go back and lick my wounds. Obviously I am struggling to get to a point of acceptance of all the nonsense that surrounds me. Even after having spent the past several years in investigating and introspecting the psychology of the self and its herd-mentality, I'm just not able to fully embody all that understanding. In the past I would laugh it off, which was in a way mocking them, but right now I don't seem to be getting anywhere.

I'm fully aware that it's all my own doing – it's my personal perspectives, that I've gathered over the past few years of whatever introspection I've done, from which I'm constantly judgemental about everything, and in the process, labelling everyone as low conscious. I have built my own theories and understanding about consciousness and therefore see almost everything as wrong, stupid and low conscious. How can I help it?! As I have built these perspectives, so will I have to undo them, if I really want to function cohesively in this world.

You may be itching to advise me to get rid of all this rubbish introspection and get back to living a normal life and to just be "happy"! Ha, you don't seem to get it. Sometimes I feel I should go even harder and double down on my "spiritual arrogance" and "superiority complex" and only worry about my own psychology and wellbeing, and live out the rest of my life in resignation and acquiescence.

How can you call yourself my friend, yet also have expectations of me? Are you a friend only if the specific conditions of friendship, as defined by you, are met? There are "friends" who get offended if one doesn't call the other. There's this constant tab-keeping of "I called you last, now it's your turn". And if you didn't call, boy, get prepared for a cold shoulder. These are supposedly good and kind people with moral values, but dare you call them unreasonable! And it's always only about them. Their conditions have to always be met, regardless of what may be happening at the other person's end. This concept of friendship is something I started to (not) understand only after spending a few years in self-enquiry and contemplation. It's like this: when two people meet each other for the first time they are like two complete strangers, and as they "hit it off" they decide to meet or chat again, and again, and again. And every time they do that, they keep adding more and more layers of conditions which are expected to be met by one or both. Generally speaking, both sides are quite oblivious of this, and keep taking each other for granted. And that's the main issue with friendships, or with any relationship for that matter.

Any relationship that is not built on a solid foundation of open-mindedness, inclusiveness and forgiveness is bound to have sustenance issues. Having said all that, I don't necessarily call myself a "good friend" in the societal sense, which is what I get in return. I understand that, but only now. But I now also understand that there's only me. Really, there's no one else, and how good a friend I am to myself could be a reasonable question to contemplate on.

Pope Francis once said that the choice to not have children is selfish. I don't fully agree. Isn't having a child in many ways being selfish? Everyone is entitled to make their own life choices that they think would work for them, whether that be to have children or not. And the reasons could be anything – time constraints, finance, career or something else. So just because you can, doesn't mean you *should* bring children into the world.

We should be able to question our own conditioning and not simply succumb to societal pressures. After all, it's a *life* that you're bringing into this world. Think about it. Have you looked into the costs and the sacrifices required to raising a child? It is very important that you responsibly think it through. Keep in mind, it's at least a 20-year full-time commitment.

I'm called a heretic, because my way of thinking, understanding and functioning is different from the majority. If I suggest ideas about how and why we should function or do things in a certain manner, that would be appreciated only from a theoretical perspective, not from an execution point of view – because you see, it's not practical or pragmatic! I'm sure, slowly but surely, most of what I'm suggesting will become the "normal" way in the not-too-distant future – that's just how evolution works.

The one factor that determines success is determination. This morning when I was meditating, every now and then I felt the urge to either move, scratch an itch or just swallow, and every time I strengthened my grit to avoid doing any of those things, my meditation became better.

When you persevere and persist, it is in the very nature of nature to support you. There's amazing power in just staying in the ring, in stick-to-itiveness. We know what to do and what not to, the only question is if we're determined enough to follow through.

What proves the concept of non-duality or *advaita* is this: there's only you, i.e the metaphysical you (life/consciousness), but you cannot exist or do anything without the body. Nor can the body do or exist without life. Hence the word *nondual*, as opposed to one or singular.

Even the root system of a computer is binary i.e. zeros and ones, but it's actually non-dual. Zero and One work in tandem, they're holonic and cannot function without each other. It's like referring to zero as nothingness, one as everythingness. I understand that I am using semantics and word play, but how else can I explain non-duality?

There is no duality in love, for love is more than an emotion, it is a state of being.

When someone is in love they say they are "in" love. Period. They might say that they're in love with someone, but in fact this love is coming from within and it's not about the "someone" they're in love with. There is no "lovee"; and when there is no lovee, there cannot be a lover and if there's no lover or lovee, then it has to imply that love is only a state of being, like joy or peace. Hence, we can only *be* in states of joy, peace and love. The feeling of being in love may have been prompted by another person, but that state of being in love is reflected upon everyone and everything, completely and thoroughly. So when one's in love, all they are is *in* love and in the mode of truly being, where any interaction with anyone or anything will carry that state. Love can only be shared, not be asked for or taken, because it is generated from within.

So you see, love is beyond any duality, it does not need or have an object or a subject.

Here's another contradiction: I may have made newage-y inferences of love and light, and that darkness is the absence of light, but come to think of it, there's only darkness. If you were to travel far into outer space, you will see that it's totally dark up there. The Milky Way, other galaxies and the universe is totally dark, and the only bits of light you'll see is that that's emanated from the sun or other stars.

We probably need setbacks, even minor ones, to really help us propel forward; especially when we're sitting comfortably and the sailing is smooth, we all of a sudden get a curveball and become unsure about what to do. But such setbacks can be used as a new starting block enabling us to adopt a fresh, more efficient and enhanced approach.

I am frustrated by other people's unawareness, but actually even more so by my own unawareness of their unawareness. I'm not saying that I am the aware one, I'm only aware that I'm unaware. And like everyone else I'm also working on becoming more conscious. I sometimes get mad at myself for just not getting it! Many consider themselves to be aware, not realising that intellectual knowledge is only a small part of this holistic awareness, which includes true understanding, open-mindedness, inclusiveness and consciousness.

As a life coach, one cannot take credit for having created any changes in the client. They just happen to be in that situation where the client is in the process of realisation. All the life coach is really doing is facilitating a situation, through questioning, where the client begins to get a fresher perspective – to be more accepting of themselves, and then to develop and progress. They now begin to broaden their awareness and realise the changes they need to make within to feel better.

Why are we happy with just the way we are and not making any effort to becoming actualised? Why don't we believe we can be as significant as people like Gandhi, Guru Nanak, Jesus, Einstein, Lao Tsu, Gautama Buddha, Mahavira or Mother Teresa? What is it that stops us from being truly significant and making a difference in the world? Is it the illusion of having knowledge that stops us? Is it our ego that stops us? Is it not seeing results quickly enough that stops us? Is it our laziness from getting up and doing something that stops us? Is it because we resist change? Is it because we're scared of change? Is it because we don't have enough courage? Is it because we don't want to fail? Is it because we don't want to succeed? Is it because we don't want to strive to succeed? Is it because we just want everything to happen without us doing anything about it?

Or is it because we don't consider ourselves part of nature? Nothing stops nature from how it operates, functions and grows. When we fully understand and truly believe with all of our intentions that we are part of nature and part of the grand intelligence, we will make our foray into awakening, actualisation and self-transcendence.

There's only one sound, only one vibration that we can generate, and that's the sound of *aa*. The other one, you could argue, is *aa* but with a closed mouth, which is *mm*. All spoken languages (sounds) of the world are only the result of the manipulation of the tongue and lips while generating the sound of *aa*. Hence, at the very core, all languages are basically the same, i.e they arise from the same source, and the millions of words are the result of how and when the tongue and lips are worked, guided and manoeuvred. As for linguistic scripts, they're only symbolic interpretations and images of those sounds.

Retirement is a state of mind. Only a few months before turning 50 did I understand that. And I took retirement, but ever since I "retired" I have been working pretty much nonstop, and I intend to keep working until the very end. Confused?!

Look, you don't have to hit any number (age/money) before you can finally hang up your boots. You can do it right now. And keep them hanging forever! Yet on the other hand, you should die with your boots on. Retirement, like almost everything else, is a mere label, and it's important to know what sort of outlook, mindset and attitude you have about it.

All of us are only concepts. Each and every living being is only a concept; it is the words or labelling that give them meaning, from a humanistic point of view. But all said and done, we're all just concepts.

When you're in traffic and someone gives you way, after many others who didn't, you only thank the one who gave you way, right?! One day on my way back from work, I realised that each of those who didn't give us way has to also be thanked, for they've all played a part in glorifying the one who actually gave way.

This metaphor can be applied to different life situations. All those who are on a "lower" level of awareness and consciousness have all contributed to the few that are on a "higher" level, yet we thank, glorify and revere only the wise ones without giving any regard to the others.

If you consider yourself reasonable and integrous, then you have to thank all situations and people that have played a part, whether directly or indirectly, in making you so. All the people in the past, all the situations of the past, whether pleasant or unpleasant, have contributed to bringing you where you are today.

There's only now, the present moment. This is truth, this is reality.

To keep the body functioning at its optimal level, pay close attention to a) food and diet, b) fitness and exercise, and c) rest and recovery. Regardless of personal aspirations, career goals, long days and hard work, if you do not include proper diet, physical exercise, and rest in your regimen, then you're neglecting a very important aspect of your life – your physiology.

Do you measure your wealth and success by how much money you have in your bank account, or by how much time you have in order to think, learn, contemplate and *be*?

You don't have to do anything for anybody or to please anyone. "So do it only for yourself?" Actually no, you don't have to do it for yourself either. You do it only because it's meant to be done. And you do it in a manner that is creative in spirit. It doesn't matter what it is that you're doing – at work, at home, with people – it's all the same.

Come to think of it, at the heart of everything I'm saying is pretty much the same thing, for they're all interlinked. I'm only using different words and expressions, and different situations to articulate the same thing. That's just the way it is, everything just comes down to one thing.

When it comes to parenting, you don't have to actively develop your child. All you as parents need to do is create an environment that is pleasant and encouraging. You don't have to constantly do things for them or always interfere in their lives. As a matter of fact, it's probably better to stay out of their way. You only need to let them know, not necessarily through your words, but just by the way you *are*, that you're always there for support. Your child is always watching and observing you, and they pick up things by how you are and behave, and what you do, rather than what you say or advise.

We live in an age of helpfulness. Most of us today are willing to provide help to others, whether that's to a friend, family member, colleague, neighbour or even to a stranger. We get excited by the opportunity to be of service to others, and we do that with enthusiasm and compassion. It gives us a sense of pride and satisfaction when we're there for others.

My question is: what would it take for us to *ask* for help? How often do we ask for help, and give others the opportunity to help us, so that they too can feel happy and fulfilled? If providing help to others makes us feel good, why don't we give others the opportunity to feel good as well? Why do we find it hard to ask for help whether that's from friends, family members or colleagues? Is it simply because we'd feel indebted to them?

What kind of a world are we living in, where asking for help is considered a sign of weakness? What are we going to do with all the pride we're so tightly holding on to, that we refuse to ask for help? Bear in mind that when all this is over, there will be people helping us with the last rites and funeral, and sadly at that point we won't be able to even thank them for that.

Inertia: A car uses maximum amount of fuel/energy when you move it from its stationary position, and as you keep accelerating, the car will not only consume less fuel, but will also run smoother. Similarly, when it comes to actualising and seeking truth, a lot of effort and energy will be required to get off the blocks, but as you persevere and keep digging deeper, you will most definitely gain momentum.

I'd like to iterate, that there's only one step, but remember that there *is* that step. What kind of inertia you apply is in your hands – taking the step is inertia of motion, not taking is inertia of rest.

Can unborn life forms die? Ridiculous question you'd say – one has to be born to die. Which also means that once birth has taken place, the other certainty is that death will also take place. So it begs the question of whether we're really living beings? Aren't we actually "dying" beings? This again proves the concept of non-duality – living and dying although linguistically opposite, are actually the same.

Sage 2.0 is one who lives like a recluse or a hermit, not by excluding, but through inclusiveness. In the past, if you wanted to become a monk or a sage, you'd need to *exclude* i.e. give up your home, family life, socialising, work, profession, money, material possessions, and perhaps go live in a cave, atop a mountain or under a tree.

The modern sage, however, lives quite in contrast – in a mode of *inclusiveness*. Sage 2.0 pursues career, family, money and comfort, yet their sense of connectedness to the infinite intelligence is honest-to-goodness.

One of the biggest problems with ideologies, intellectualism and even scientism is that everything can be simply reduced to something, least of all to atoms and particles. That's nothing but oversimplifying reality and not doing, worse still, not willing to do any epistemic research to understand the complexities of life, and the metaphysical nature of the universe. However, when we view life and the universe deeply enough, we will see that everything is holonic and irreducible. Absolutely everything including everyone is interconnected.

The seven sins are pride, greed, wrath, envy, lust, gluttony and sloth. Conversely, the seven virtues are prudence, justice, temperance, courage, faith, hope and charity. And whilst both lists are polar opposites of each other, they are both equally important to be understood and appreciated. Wanting or being one but not the other is a very dualistic way of living.

Advaitha or non-duality is acknowledging both, including both, being both, staying detached from both and transcending both – remembering that as much as the two may appear contradictory, they're actually complementary.

Religious books and scriptures may suggest you to be virtuous and not sinful, which is probably a good starting place, where you live, breathe and exist all the time in the space of those virtues. However, once you're able to sustain that space consistently for long enough, there will occur a shift within your consciousness, when you begin to understand transcendence. That's when life begins. You're born again.

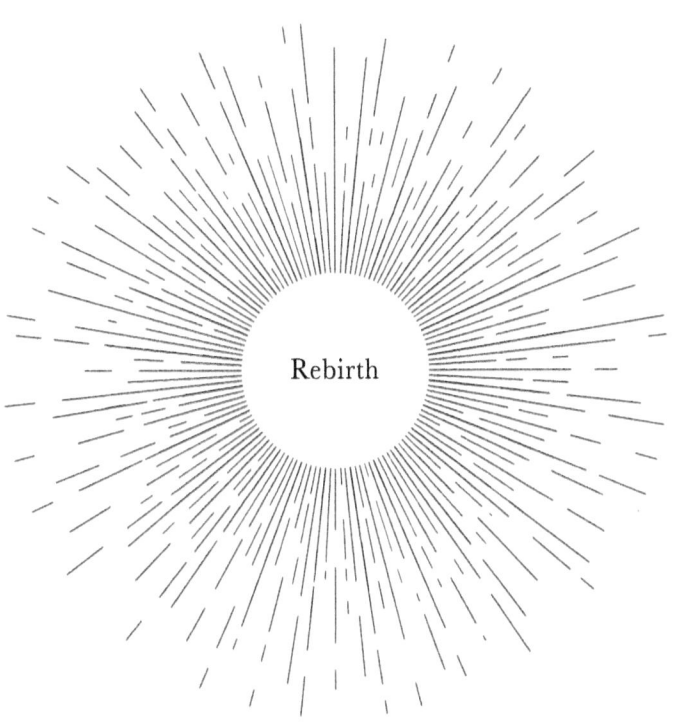

Life is a journey – from cradle to grave. And everything in it, including all learning, success, failure, happiness, delusion and awakening are aspects of this pilgrimage. And it's not possible to arrive at any destination without going through the journey.

Just like in tennis. Come to think of it, tennis uses the language of life: advantage, service, fault, break, love etc. Even the structure of tennis, the way the pieces fit inside one another, mimics the structure of journey and time – points become games become sets become matches become tournaments. Like how seconds become minutes become hours become days and so on. If someone like RF won Wimbledon, he wouldn't have won, had he not journeyed through the championship point, the previous games, the previous sets, semifinals, quarterfinals, going all the way back to the very first point of the first game of the first set of the first round. Can you see that playing every point is in itself a journey, and winning a point is arriving at a mini destination? There's one important aspect here, which is about being courageous and taking risks. You cannot win a championship by being risk-averse and only hitting to the middle of the court; you have to go for low percentage shots and sidelines, and the more chances you take and expand your comfort zone, the more chances of you winning. Tennis is only one sport. Every sport can be deconstructed, broken down and used as a metaphor for life. But not just sport; every endeavour can be philosophised using the journey vs destination metaphor. How we deal with the course and all its obstacles will determine how effectively and efficiently we arrive at the destination – only to start a new journey to a new destination.

As this is reaching the end, I feel a bit lost – what has kept me busy and involved for almost a year is nearing the finish line. Although writing and journaling has always been part of my entire life, barring a couple of decades in the middle, putting together some of the content has been truly enjoyable. As I leave you, I'd like to suggest to you an affirmation: *Any identity is finite, but I am infinite.* Introspect, contemplate and meditate on this one concept, and your everyday life will become so much more meaningful and profound, that it will bring you to tears.

As for meditation, it is one of the best tools, if not the best tool, to ground oneself into "this here now". Although I got into meditating many years ago, I didn't start reaping all its benefits until I made it a diligent daily practice.

If I can sum up what this entire journey is all about, then it's as follows: increasing awareness and knowledge, becoming less egotistical and selfish, always siding with Truth, overcoming "threshold guardians", all in order to become fully enlightened.

Our only purpose is to become, not just somewhat, but *fully* enlightened. However, we're in denial of this, for it's buried somewhere deep within our subconscious. We therefore need to fully acknowledge the one and only purpose of our existence, then pursue it, without dismissing it for anything else, no matter what that may be.

The word *love* is one of most commonly used words in the English language, yet I feel the true essence of it isn't being fully understood. The Universe, the Cosmos, and Nature are constantly providing us evidence of how everything functions in a space of love and synergy. And the universal intelligence is constantly organising everything perfectly out of universal love, which a lot of us miss seeing and experiencing, because of our conditioning and limited perspectives.

The poet Hafiz said: *Even after all this time, the Sun never says to the Earth, "you owe me"; look what happens with a love like that, it lights up the whole sky*.

There is only love in this world, there is no hate. Hate is nothing but absence of love. Love is not the absence of hate – love is always present. Like how there's only light – darkness is the absence of light, light is not the absence of darkness. This is a very important concept to fully comprehend, for it could become the basis of all illusion, and could help resolve many issues and errors. We believe, or are made to believe, that there is evil and negativity, but in truth there isn't any. It is we who choose to see things in the way that is inconsistent with all the love, kindness and peace that's around us. At our very essence, we are all "good" and aligned with nature. We *choose* to move away from our soul, our inner goodness and take on our fears and our neuroses, and to live each day without passion and enthusiasm for life.

Love is giving, not expecting. What in the world gives us any right to expect love? "Expecting love" is an oxymoron, because expectation is related to getting, and love to giving. The receiving of love is not within our control, whereas giving is. Having said that, the law of reciprocity somehow works in the case of love, for as we give love, so we receive. Keeping in mind though, that the giving is not done with the intention of receiving. The one thing, the only thing we have unchallengeable control over is in our capacity to show, provide and give love.

Wholehearted love is what it's all about, also referred to as unconditional love – love that is complete, total and absolute. The kind of love that is loving each and every -one and -thing equally. Equally! Whether that's to oneself, a parent, a partner, a spouse, a child, a friend, a sibling, a grandparent, a grandchild, a cousin, an in-law, a teacher, a student, an uncle, an aunt, a pet, a colleague, a classmate, a manager, a subordinate, a competitor or opponent, a tree, a plant, a book, a mobile phone, the sun, the rain, the wind, the traffic, a beverage, sickness, wellness, a disease, adversity, failure, a loss, food, an animal, a bird, an insect, a car, a bike and everything else. And it's also about loving them in all of their expressions – whether they're happy, sad, proud, greedy, angry, peaceful, lazy, jealous, vulnerable, hurtful, courageous, joyful, nasty, shameful, guilty, indifferent, prejudiced or any other emotion.

Make becoming fully enlightened your only vision or goal. Think less, and be in the present moment – as much as possible. Understand that there's only you/I, i.e. there's only the individual Self. Accept and include all aspects of you, especially whatever you consider "negative".

Life, and everything in it, is unbelievably complex and sophisticated, and it cannot be articulated using any language – like the map can never be the territory. The territory can be depicted with a map, but it can only be experienced with awe, veneration and wonder. With that said, and to put it simply, there's *only* you, which is the ultimate Truth. Not the ego you, but the divine you. And when I say you, I really mean you personally, the individual Self – that's the only Truth.

There are two main aspects to this Truth – the tangible and the intangible. And they're holons – your mind and your body are as much wholes as they're parts of the whole, and cannot do without each other. A very large part of the metaphysical you is the result of the physical you, and vice versa; and they're both consequences of your physical environment and your mental experiences. Your mind can be the result of your philosophy, intellect, fears, emotions, insecurities, beliefs, likes, dislikes, experiences, education, knowledge and psychology; and your body the result of the food and drinks you've consumed, the physical exercises and movements you've done and the stillness and rest you've given it.

I don't need to tell you much about meditation, as in how to do it or what its benefits are, but what I will suggest is to make it a practice. Important: It's not about how long you do it for, but how often. For example, you could do one session for one hour, or 3 sessions of 20 minutes spread through the day, or 5 x 10-minute sessions – like doing a *Salah/Namaaz*. If you're religious and go to the temple, church or mosque to pray once a week, just imagine the transformation you'd have if you were to pray many times each day!

Meditation can really help you understand the profundity of life – to know if you're truly living life or merely staying alive. We're always responding, all the time. Meditation is probably the best way to not respond. Or in other words, it's the best way *to* respond, however with stillness and with silence. No matter what you encounter or what happens to you, you meditate. Something good happens, you meditate; something bad happens, you meditate. Your spouse, parent, child, colleague, friend or anyone says or does something hurtful or nice, you meditate. You're busy with activities, you take time out to meditate. You structure your entire day around meditation. Meditation is your life, everything else fits around it.

If you fan the flames too strongly then you will put out the fire. If you fan it too gently it won't do anything. However, if you fan it properly with the right intensity and strength, you will help it become stronger.

Each of us has the ability to find that spark within ourselves and in others. And once we see that spark, or even a little flicker, let's do everything possible to help it become a raging fire – so that it can burn freely, like the sun.

Well, it's a wrap! Almost 43,000 words, that's a lot! Goodonya for making it to the end, for resisting all your urges to put it down much earlier. I applaud and commend you for staying curious and reading it through. I'm reminded of a quote by Mark Twain: *"I didn't have time to write you a short letter, so I wrote you a long one."* I may have bombarded you with so many words, but I must say that had I put together this journal or memoir a few years ago, it would have been twice as thick as this one. So I have definitely put in a lot of effort and thought on the brevity of this book.

Anyways, I trust that you've been able to get a gist of where I'm coming from. You may conclude that all I've done here is play word games, and use metaphors to write this book. That is not true. As much as I've used language to verbalise my thoughts and ideas, the basis of anything I may have suggested is for the reader to go beyond the words and to directly experience them. Direct experience is *king*, it is the Truth.

I'm not sure if you picked up on this, but two of the most frequently used words in this "thesis" of mine – the obvious ones aside – are Life and Consciousness. Think about that.

Lastly, as I wind up, I want to give a huge and massive shout-out to the girls for helping me bring this work into fruition, and for all their help with the editing and proofreading, aside from softening and moderating some of the content. A special mention to my daughter who, having already self-published two of her own books (I'm following in her footsteps :-)), has also helped me with the cover design and artwork. *Ummmmas* to them.

www.ingramcontent.com/pod-product-compliance
Lightning Source LLC
Chambersburg PA
CBHW030252010526
44107CB00053B/1670